STEP

SYSTEMATIC TRAINING FOR EFFECTIVE PARENTING

Leader's Manual

Don Dinkmeyer, Ph.D.
Gary D. McKay, Ph.D.

AGS ®
American Guidance Service
Circle Pines, Minnesota 55014-1796

®

Second edition ©1989 AGS® American Guidance Service, Inc.
First edition©1976

A   10   9   8   7   6   5   4   3

ISBN 0-88671-299-8

Contents

Acknowledgments

Systematic Training for Effective Parenting (STEP) is an educational program for parents who want to raise responsible children and to feel more adequate and satisfied as parents.

The STEP program was developed over a period of years, was subjected to intensive field testing, and now serves millions of parents. The following people are some who have contributed to the development of the program:

We particularly want to recognize the influence of Dr. Rudolf Dreikurs and the professional staff of the Alfred Adler Institute of Chicago. Their instruction, stimulation, and encouragement provided us many insights into parent-child relationships.

Dr. Thomas Allen, Office of Student Development, Washington University, St. Louis, Missouri, and Dr. Jon Carlson, Lake Geneva Wellness Center, Lake Geneva, Wisconsin, who reviewed and critiqued the *Leader's Manual* and *The Parent's Handbook,* thereby assisting in the development of the program.

Robert Kraske, Stillwater, Minnesota, and Alice Cecil, West Bend, Wisconsin, who assisted in the early editorial development of the material.

Dr. Jwalla Somwaru, Alexandra Robbin, and Karen Dahlen, for their much-valued critical and editorial contributions to the program.

David Youngquist, who coordinated development and production of the original STEP kit and its components.

Dr. James Straub and Dr. Vicki Straub, Columbia, Missouri, and Dr. Bill Hillman, University of Arizona, Tucson, who supplied feedback and suggestions during the early stages of program development.

Dr. Joyce L. McKay, Vice President of the Communication and Motivation Training Institute-West, Tucson, Arizona, for her personal and professional assistance, encouragement, and valued feedback to the authors.

Dr. Norman Bloss, Barbara Barkenbush, and Jody Burns of the Pima County Developmental Career Guidance Project, who contributed their time and talents to the coordination of the Tucson field test.

Dr. Don Dinkmeyer, Jr., who reviewed art, tapescripts, and manuscript revisions for the 1989 edition of the program.

Eleanor Yackel, Circle Pines, Minnesota, whose careful reading and suggestions provided guidance for the authors.

Sally Laufketter, St. Louis, Missouri, who not only field-tested the material, but also provided a constructive and creative critique.

E. Jane Dinkmeyer, who not only demonstrated effective parenting, but also provided typing, feedback, encouragement, and patience as needed.

The school counselors and volunteer instructors from various parts of North America who provided valuable feedback and critiques regarding their experiences with the field-test edition of the program.

Finally, we would like to thank the many parents and leaders who have participated in both the field test and the published program. Their interest, responses, and enthusiasm have encouraged us and have helped bring the message of STEP into homes throughout the world.

Don Dinkmeyer
Gary D. McKay
March, 1989

Introduction

People need training to become effective parents. In the past, the only qualification thought to be needed was biological. But now things are different. Our society is undergoing rapid social change. We are living in an era of increasing social equality in which people are refusing to be treated as inferior. Recent movements toward social equality—women with men, children with adults—have presented challenges that most parents are not prepared to meet. We need to learn to live with each other as equals.

The "democratic revolution" has rendered the autocratic approach inappropriate and ineffective. As a result, the traditional way of disciplining children—by reward and punishment—needs to be reconsidered. Reward and punishment as a method of control fits only an autocratic society and an autocratic home.

Traditional methods of raising children are failing to achieve what parents want most: responsible children who grow into responsible men and women. To achieve the desired goal, we need new approaches to the raising of children—namely, new parent-child relationships. Since social equality is becoming a reality, these new relationships need to be based on democratic principles.

What is a democratic process for bringing up children? In contrast to autocratic child-rearing methods—in which the parents make and enforce rules and the children submit—democratic child-rearing methods are based on mutual respect and equality. The term "equality" is often misunderstood. We do not use it in the sense of equal attributes. Instead, we are using the term as it applies to human worth and dignity.

We assume that each person in a family is entitled to equal respect. We believe that parents should provide opportunities for children to make decisions, within limits, and should allow them to be responsible for their decisions. This type of guidance is called "natural and logical consequences." It replaces reward and punishment as a method of disciplining children.

Democratic parents learn to communicate with their children and to encourage them. Communication and encouragement imply valuing each child as an individual who deserves love and respect.

But parents don't just happen to become democratic parents; they become that way deliberately. Hence, the purpose of this course is to help parents discard outmoded methods of raising children and become able to meet the challenges of raising children in a democratic society.

Why STEP?

Parents are constantly exposed to advice—some unsolicited—on how to raise their children. Pediatricians give it and so do relatives, friends, neighbors, magazine writers, and newspaper columnists.

To replace this barrage of often conflicting information, STEP—*Systematic Training for Effective Parenting*—offers parents a practical alternative to meet the challenges of raising children today.

STEP is intended for study group use because the program's authors have found study groups an especially effective method for parent education. In a group, parents provide encouragement for each other. They share concerns and soon learn that their problems are not unique. Through discussions, they become aware that their own reactions and attitudes may have influenced their children's unacceptable behaviors.

More specifically, STEP helps parents learn effective ways to relate to their children. By clarifying the purposes of children's behavior, STEP also helps parents learn how not to reinforce their children's unacceptable behaviors and how to encourage cooperative behavior.

Through STEP, parents discover something else of great value—that they are not necessarily the cause of difficulties with their children. When this burden of guilt is removed, parents are freed to function more effectively.

Other parenting programs available that use the STEP approach are STEP/Teen, which addresses the special challenges of parenting teenagers, and *The Next STEP*, a follow-up program for parents who have taken STEP or STEP/Teen and want additional training.

Development and Field Testing

Systematic Training for Effective Parenting (STEP) underwent development and revision over a period of two years. In the fall of 1974, a full-scale field test was carried out among 14 parent study groups in the states of Arizona, Florida, Minnesota, and Missouri. Feedback from these study groups led to the first published version of STEP in 1976.

Results of research done on STEP since its publication in 1976 are available from the Instructional Materials Department, American Guidance Service, Publishers' Building, P.O. Box 99, Circle Pines, MN 55014-1796.

Leader Qualifications

A STEP parent education group can be led by a person trained in the helping professions—psychology, social work, counseling, the ministry, pediatrics, education, nursing, psychiatry. It can also be led by a lay person who is willing to study this manual intensively and has the ability to lead discussion groups. A STEP leader doesn't have to be an authority on child training. The leader arranges the program for each session, starts each lesson, and facilitates group discussion. The program itself serves as the authority.

Materials

Contained in an easy-to-carry box, the STEP kit includes:

One *Leader's Manual.* The *Leader's Manual* includes an introduction to the program, information on organizing and leading a STEP parent study group, and guidelines for leading group discussion. It also includes detailed session plans.

One *Parent's Handbook.* This colorful, cartoon-illustrated book contains readings and exercises in principles of democratic parent-child relations. Each participant is to have a personal copy of the book; one copy of the handbook is included in each kit. The handbook also includes:

> **Problem Situations.** The Problem Situations are examples of child-rearing problems for discussion during sessions. These situations help the group generalize and integrate the concepts presented in each lesson.

> **Charts.** Ten charts summarize the major concepts and principles of the STEP program. They are reproductions of the large charts used during group sessions.

> **Points to Remember.** A list of each session's major points is included in each chapter of the handbook. Parents may want to cut it out and post it at home, perhaps on a bulletin board or the refrigerator.

> **My Plan for Improving Relationships.** Each chapter in the handbook includes a form on which parents can privately plan and assess their progress in dealing with specific parent-child relationships. Parents can also cut out this form.

Two Videocassettes *or* Five Audiocassettes. A recorded video or audio segment is presented in each STEP session. These segments illustrate typical parent-child situations and show how STEP principles and procedures can be used effectively in these situations. The video or audio serves to stimulate discussion during sessions. The leader is signaled at certain points to stop the tape and conduct related discussions or exercises.

One *Script Booklet.* Transcripts and discussion questions for the recorded video and audio segments are included in the *Script Booklet.*

One Discussion Guidelines Poster. This poster illustrating the principles of effective discussion is introduced in the first session and displayed during each session.

Ten Charts. Ten large charts summarize the program's major concepts and principles. The charts are displayed during sessions and are also printed in *The Parent's Handbook.*

Twenty-Five Certificates of Participation. Certificates of Participation can be given to participants upon completion of the STEP course. Additional certificates can be purchased from the publisher.

Publicity Aids. Included in your STEP kit are publicity aids to help you promote your program. Contained in an envelope, the materials include an announcement poster, 25 invitational fliers, and a set of reproducible aids including camera-ready ad slicks, public service announcement, and a news release. Also provided are instructions for using the aids.

Additional help in organizing a STEP parent study group is provided by an introductory segment of the audiocassette and videocassette called "Introduction to STEP." It describes the STEP program and can be used to stimulate interest in joining your group.

STEP Program Overview

Session	Leader's Manual	Chart	Audiocassettes	Videocassettes	Parent's Handbook
1	Understanding Children's Behavior and Misbehavior	1A. The Goals of Misbehavior 1B. The Goals of Positive Behavior	Cassette 1, Side B The Four Goals of Misbehavior	Videocassette 1 The Four Goals of Misbehavior	Understanding Children's Behavior and Misbehavior
2	Understanding How Children Use Emotions to Involve Parents *and* The "Good" Parent	2. Differences Between the "Good" Parent and the Responsible Parent	Cassette 2, Side A Emotions Serve a Purpose	Videocassette 1 Emotions Serve a Purpose	Understanding More about Your Child and about Yourself as a Parent
3	Encouragement	3. Differences Between Praise and Encouragement	Cassette 2, Side B Encouragement	Videocassette 1 Encouragement	Encouragement: Building Your Child's Confidence and Feelings of Worth
4	Communication: Listening	4. Effective Listening	Cassette 3, Side A Effective Listening	Videocassette 1 Effective Listening	Communication: How to Listen to Your Child
5	Communication: Exploring Alternatives and Expressing Your Ideas and Feelings to Children	5. Decisions for Effective Communication	Cassette 3, Side B Problem Ownership and I-Messages	Videocassette 2 Problem Ownership and I-Messages	Communication: Exploring Alternatives and Expressing Your Ideas and Feelings to Children
6	Developing Responsibility	6. The Major Differences Between Punishment and Logical Consequences	Cassette 4, Side A Creating Logical Consequences	Videocassette 2 Creating Logical Consequences	Natural and Logical Consequences: A Method of Discipline That Develops Responsibility
7	Decision Making for Parents	7. Selecting the Appropriate Approach	Cassette 4, Side B Disciplining with Consequences	Videocassette 2 Disciplining with Consequences	Applying Natural and Logical Consequences to Other Concerns
8	The Family Meeting	8. Essentials of Family Meetings	Cassette 5, Side A The Family Meeting	Videocassette 2 The Family Meeting	The Family Meeting
9	Developing Confidence and Using Your Potential	9. Democratic and Positive Parenting	Cassette 5, Side B Building Your Confidence	Videocassette 2 Building Your Confidence	Developing Confidence and Using Your Potential

11

Part One
STEP Group Leadership

Why Study Groups for Parents?*

The family is the most significant influence on the development of the individual. Our values, attitudes, and perceptions of life are influenced by the quality of our relationships with our parents, by the training procedures our parents used, and by our position in our family constellation.

The influence of the family on the child is generally acknowledged, but only in recent years has the question been raised: Do parents need training to raise their children?

We require barbers, taxicab drivers, accountants, electricians, and real estate brokers to be trained and certified, but "anyone can be a parent." It appears that we must be very careful about who cuts our hair or keeps our books or wires our home, but that raising children can be left to chance. An increasing percentage of our children are underachieving, uncooperative, and apparently unhappy. If parenting is left a haphazard process, we can expect a continuation of these trends.

Some parents will protest our viewpoint that parents need training: "*My* parents had no formal training, and they did all right. Why the sudden need to train people to raise children?"

To answer this question, it is important to consider the revolutionary social changes that have occurred within a single generation.

Most of today's parents were raised in autocratic families. When their own parents asked them to do something—"Pick up your clothes, please"—the request was accepted as a command. The children may have resisted and resented it, but in the end they complied. Parents were considered superior; children had little choice but to obey. For a child to question a parent's request was considered disrespectful; compliance was expected. Not all homes were monarchies, of course, but even in the more lenient there was an authoritarian atmosphere that enabled parents to control their children.

Do parents control their children today?

Most of us would answer no. Parents, responding to a number of influences in society—including some well-intentioned but faulty child-training advice—are frequently ineffective. More permissive attitudes have gained acceptance. The vacuum created when parents lost their socially sanctioned position of power has been filled by the tyranny of children. We need only to watch unruly children or to note the lack of communication between parents and children in order to recognize that neither permissiveness nor autocracy is working effectively.

Today, parents are an unrepresented minority group. Following the sociopolitical changes effected by women and minority groups in recent years, parents and children remain adrift in their struggles for identity and human equality. The swing from yesterday's autocracy to today's permissive society has left both parents and children confused.

---

*Note: The term *parent* will be used to refer to any person functioning in that role.

Unfortunately, most people do not understand the democratic assumptions that underlie mutual respect, equality, rights, and responsibilities for both parents and children. Until parents have acknowledged the bankruptcy of both autocratic and permissive approaches, they are not motivated to study and become trained in a new approach. Group leaders will need to help parents understand the failures of the bankrupt approaches so that parents will want to reconsider their usual roles. The leader needs only to ask, "Is what you're doing working?" to bring about this realization.

Currently, many families seem to fall into one or two extreme categories: autocracy or anarchy—excessive order or no order at all. Such families tend to raise either overly dependent children or tyrants who demand special privileges. In the STEP program, parents come to understand the necessity of establishing a democratic atmosphere in which they are kind but firm and in which all family members are treated with equal respect. The goal requires study and training—which the STEP program provides.

The objectives of parent study groups are to help parents

- Understand a practical theory of human behavior and its implications for parent-child relationships.
- Learn new procedures for establishing democratic relationships with their children.
- Improve communication between themselves and their children so all concerned feel they are being heard.
- Develop skills of listening, resolving conflicts, and exploring alternatives with their children.
- Learn how to use encouragement and logical consequences to modify their children's self-defeating motives and behaviors.
- Learn how to conduct family meetings.
- Become aware of their own self-defeating patterns and faulty convictions which keep them from being effective parents who enjoy their children.

How to Organize and Conduct a STEP Parent Study Group

Today there is a growing interest among parents to find more effective ways of relating to their children. In cities across the United States and Canada, parents have joined organized study groups. The federal government supports parent education classes in schools. In some areas parent education is conducted as part of the regular adult education program in the community. Many parents are becoming actively involved in programs for changing their relationships with their children.

Although there is a ready supply of clients for parent education, it is very important for someone who wants to organize a group to use a systematic approach. Your first contact might be made at a public or social gathering, such as a home-and-school or church meeting. At this meeting, you could present reasons for forming parent study groups and include some important principles for the listeners to consider. Two topics that usually interest parents are the four goals of misbehavior (as set forth in the first chart) and the use of logical consequences (as described in Chapter 6 of *The Parent's Handbook*).

At this meeting, play the introductory segment from the audiotape or videotape. Then distribute the STEP invitational fliers, which explain reasons for the parent study groups, list objectives, and state what parents can expect to gain from participating in such a group.

Tell parents that the group is for discussion and practice in developing skills that are essential to good parent-child relationships. Explain that members will be expected to do some home activities in the form of skill practice and reading. Emphasize that they are to come to meetings prepared to exchange ideas with each other.

Take care to point out that participation in a parent discussion group does not suggest inadequacy—that on the contrary, it indicates a desire to grow and recognizes the importance of learning new procedures for raising children. Emphasize that the study group will deal with normal challenges of typical parents, not with psychological problems of troubled children. Be sure to clarify that the group is *not designed for group therapy* or for the handling of behavior problems that require intensive professional assistance.

While you explain the purpose of the parent discussion group, have available a sign-up sheet for names, addresses, and phone numbers of interested people. At the top of the sheet indicate the dates, hour, and place of the planned meetings.

If a school decides to recruit parents for a study group, you may want to suggest inviting parents of children in a particular grade. The principal might ask a teacher to send notices home, and perhaps a room parent could make follow-up phone calls.

Limit the first group to a size that will permit all members to participate in discussions. Usually 10 to 12, plus the leader, is an effective number. If you get more enrollees than the specified maximum, run two groups or develop a waiting list for another group rather than start with a group too large to be led effectively. Latecomers can form another group.

Members are to understand from the beginning that they are making a commitment to attend all nine sessions. Of course, if a participant does not feel at ease with the program, an opportunity should be given for withdrawing without embarrassment.

Preparing for the STEP Study Group

1. Physical Setting. Choose a location that will assure privacy. Members must feel free to raise concerns without having to compete with distractions or intrusions. The place must be quiet enough for participants to hear the tapes and each other.

Chairs should be comfortable. Circular placement is preferred. Such an arrangement implies the equal importance of all members, including the leader. Circular seating tends to break down the idea that the leader is superior, an authority, while the members are inferior, uninformed. It is also easier to conduct open discussions when every person can see the face of everyone else.

If the room does not permit circular seating, arrange a semicircular or a rectangular format. Group members must be able to see each other's faces.

2. Time. The hour of the meeting, of course, is dictated by the schedules of the potential members and of the leader. It may be most convenient for parents who do not work outside the home to attend meetings while their children are in school. If the meeting is held at a school, the older children in the building may be allowed to assist in the care of preschoolers during the meeting.

Evening meetings are usually more convenient for parents employed outside the home. In some areas study groups are conducted as part of the regular adult education program in the community.

3. Length of Session. The nine STEP sessions are work sessions. Inform yourself of the relative importance of the various activities and schedule the time so that members can report on their activities, discuss the reading, listen to the recordings, engage in the exercises, role-play, consider the problem situations, and summarize their impressions. The typical session will take one-and-a-half to two hours if the leader keeps things moving. Some groups who have more time available can extend the discussions and exercises to two-and-a-half hours.

4. Frequency. STEP groups generally meet once a week. This allows time between meetings for members to read *The Parent's Handbook,* to consider the relevance of its ideas for their own needs, and to make specific applications of the ideas suggested in the activity assignments. Some STEP groups have met twice a week; however, experience indicates that parents have difficulty absorbing and applying the ideas this fast.

5. Sequence of Lessons. Although we have arranged the topics of STEP in a recommended sequence, the sequence can be varied. If your experience or the composition of your group indicates that another sequence would be more appropriate, change the order to fit your situation.

6. Size of Group. Benefits from the program are greatest when every member can

- Raise questions about content.
- Participate in the exercises and skill training.
- Report on the week's activities.
- Summarize what he or she has learned and intends to do.

To permit this amount of involvement, groups should be restricted to 10 to 12 members. Objectives of the program require that all members have to participate fully.

7. Attendance. At the first meeting, emphasize that attendance at every session is expected. Participants should state a commitment to attend each session. We do not believe additional members should be accepted after the first meeting has been held. The process of getting acquainted, becoming oriented and understanding procedures, and explaining the basic theory cannot be repeated.

When a member has missed a session, encourage the person to listen to the audiocassette or watch the videocassette in order to understand what was covered in the session. If you have parents who do not read well in your group, you may want to permit them to listen to or watch the tapes on their own.

8. Refreshments. Refreshments contribute to informality and should be considered if they do not add unnecessarily to the work of the leader. Often members will share responsibility for providing refreshments. Of course, the refreshments should be only supplementary to the program and should not be used to turn the session into a social discussion.

9. Preparation Time. To be effective, you must allow yourself time to become acquainted with the entire program. This requires understanding reasons for parent study groups and how to organize and conduct them. It requires knowledge of the theory of understanding the child.

It will be helpful for you to read Dinkmeyer and McKay's *Raising a Responsible Child.** This book thoroughly covers the theory and techniques which undergird the STEP program.

Obviously, you must listen to the tapes and understand the exercises and assignments and the content of *The Parent's Handbook* before starting each session.

It is important to arrive early at the session to make sure the seating arrangement is satisfactory or to rearrange chairs. Early arrival also provides time for organizing and displaying materials.

10. Materials. It is important to have a copy of *The Parent's Handbook* for each group member. A videocassette player or audiocassette tape player in good working condition is needed at each meeting. You will also want to have this manual, the appropriate chart, the *Script Booklet*, and the Discussion Guidelines Poster as well as any other materials listed at the beginning of the session.

The First Session

1. Preparation. Read all of the introductory material in this manual so you are familiar with the leadership role and the skills necessary for conducting the program. Review the specific objectives for the session. Read Chapter 1 in *The Parent's Handbook* so you understand the content and the questions. Play the tape to become familiar with the content and the exercises. Arrange the room for circular seating. Display the Discussion Guidelines Poster and have the videocassette player or audiocassette player ready with the appropriate tape. Have available a copy of *The Parent's Handbook* for each member and any other materials required for the session.

2. Introduction. Begin the first session by introducing yourself, stating the objectives of the program, and outlining the procedures that will be used.

3. Get Acquainted. At the first session, have all members give their names and the names and ages of their children in descending order, from oldest to youngest. Ask each member to repeat the names of all the other people in the group so that everyone can become acquainted on a first-name basis. Then give

*Don Dinkmeyer and Gary D. McKay, *Raising a Responsible Child* (New York: Simon and Schuster, 1973).

each member a 3" x 5" card on which to indicate his or her name, address, and phone number, plus the names and ages of the children from oldest to youngest. Keep the cards for use as a reference.

4. Assessment. Ask what the members expect to get from the meetings. (Note: During Sessions 2-9, ask members how effectively the sessions are meeting their needs.) Remind them that STEP groups are for exchanging ideas and developing skills and that the leader will not try to solve personal family problems. As the members learn the principles and practice the skills, they will be able to apply what they have learned to their individual situations.

5. Guidelines. Indicate to the members that they will learn by participating in the development of their own goals as well as in the development of group goals. Encourage all to participate and point out the disadvantages of a monologue or dialogue. From the beginning, it's important to establish a democratic leadership. The Discussion Guidelines Poster, which is explained at the first meeting and prominently displayed at the ensuing meetings, will help guide the discussions.

General Directions for the Sessions

The STEP program has been organized systematically. It is our belief that parent education can be effective only if it helps parents understand the purposes of behavior, the encouragement process, effective communication, the application of logical consequences, and the benefits of the family meeting. Therefore each session is planned to present basic principles and to provide opportunities to practice the skills necessary for effective parenting. Time is taken to discuss the reading, tapes, and charts. There is an opportunity to report on successes and difficulties in applying the activity assignments, and an opportunity to clarify what each member is learning.

Members will learn best by expressing what the concepts mean for them and their families. This will require meaningful discussion of the major concepts set forth in the objectives of each session. In addition, the ideas *must be applied* through the activity assignments if the members are to gain maximum benefit from the sessions. The leader can help clarify the principles when parents do not seem able to apply them. *We want* members to learn new ideas and to integrate the ideas into their family relationships by changing their behavior. Involvement, commitment, understanding, and application are essential if real learning is to occur. Our goal is not only to introduce ideas, but also to help parents develop skill in applying the concepts.

Group members learn most easily when leaders are able to model the process of effective parenting. For example, leaders are to avoid being "good" parents and doing for members what they can do for themselves. Instead, "I-messages" and problem ownership (as described in Chapter 5 of *The Parent's Handbook*) are used when problems arise in the group. The leader asks members to talk directly to each other with I-messages and to determine who owns the problem.

Many parents are ineffective because they lack self-confidence and a feeling of worth as parents. It is important that the leader continually encourage group members by helping them to inventory their assets and to recognize their own progress. For example: "You were more patient this time," or "You are gaining insight into the purpose of Freddy's tantrums." Parents can learn the process of encouragement from an optimistic, positive leader who is able to see each person's potential and progress. The effective leader is ready to comment on the effective way an activity assignment was handled, instead of mentioning what was not accomplished.

Specific Directions for the Sessions

Each session will typically follow this sequence:

Statement of Objectives. The session begins with an overview of what the parents will be learning. The *Leader's Manual* contains a brief statement of purpose that can be read or paraphrased.

Discussion Guidelines Poster. The guidelines are discussed at the first session and thereafter are posted as reminders.

1. Discussion of Previous Week's Activity Assignment. Near the end of each session, an assignment is made for the coming week. It is important for the leader to create an expectation that all members will complete the assignment. Do this by asking members to share their experiences and by encouraging any positive efforts or evidence of progress. Parents who are discouraged about their effectiveness can receive encouragement *for their efforts* to carry out activity assignments. Allow time for all to describe their experiences. Solicit comments from members who do not volunteer. (Note: Some may not even try the assignments because they anticipate failure or do not have the courage to be imperfect. Briefly discuss how self-defeating attitudes—for example, "I cannot succeed" or "I will do something only if I can do it very well"—can keep one from growing. Discuss how mistakes can be used as feedback to help a person learn.)

Be alert to the tendency of some members to turn this part of the session into a rationalization of their failures. Generalizations (such as, "All children are that way") are not acceptable responses in the STEP program. Help the members focus on progress.

Although discussion of the activity assignment is valuable, its time allotment should be limited. The STEP program is not merely a review of applied ideas. Too much time devoted to this activity will prevent members from obtaining other benefits from the program.

2. Discussion of Assigned Reading. The reading in *The Parent's Handbook* is to acquaint members with the concepts to be presented in the session. Begin discussion with open questions: "What did you learn from this reading, and how would you apply these ideas?" Or, "Do you have any questions about the reading?" Pick up on members' questions and concerns. Because it is important to maintain an atmosphere in which all feel free to express themselves, assure participants that there are no "dumb" questions.

Creation of a questioning atmosphere requires the leader to be patient. Do not rush. Instead, pause and scan the group to see whether any members are giving nonverbal indications that they are puzzled by some feelings or are unclear about a concept. You can encourage participation by reminding members that they can help the group as well as themselves by asking questions. Assure them that their questions are usually shared by others.

If the group is reluctant to begin, you might vary the approach by asking, "What idea particularly interested you?" or "Did you read anything you disagreed with?"

If this is ineffective, you can refer to the *Leader's Manual* for the questions that accompany the session. The questions are merely guidelines and should not restrict the discussion. If necessary, rephrase the questions. Avoid creating a typical classroom atmosphere in which members anticipate that you are the authority and that they are being tested. As in all other facets of the program, encourage any positive efforts to raise and answer questions. (Note: Leaders will find the sections on "Eight Study Group Leader Skills," "Guidelines for Discussion Leaders," and "Problems of Group Leadership" valuable resources for the discussion of assigned readings.)

3. Charts. The charts are visual aids that set forth the major concepts and principles of the program. There is a different chart for each session. The chart is displayed during the session and is used to emphasize and clarify major concepts. After the group has discussed the illustrated principles, the charts are left on display as handy references for the rest of the session.

4. Presentation of Videocassette or Audiocassette. To be sure your videocassette player or audiocassette player is functioning and to become familiar with the tape content and the activities you will lead, play the tape during your preparation period before each session. If you want to preview but do not have the necessary equipment available, the tapescript can be found in the *Script Booklet*.

Be prepared to stop the tape when signalled to do so and lead a discussion. Questions for discussion appear in the *Script Booklet* at the pertinent point in the tapescript.*

5. Discussion of the Tape. At the conclusion of the tape, group members have an opportunity to discuss its contents. This is a time for open discussion, not a time to question members. In the Discussion of the Tape section in the *Leader's Manual*, there is a list of major ideas which the leader can check to see if there is need for further clarification.

6. Exercises and Role-Plays. These exercises, many of them found in *The Parent's Handbook,* simulate parent-child interaction so that parents can practice the essential STEP skills. Make every effort to organize the exercises so all members have an opportunity to participate.

---

*Leaders familiar with the audiorecordings in the original edition of the STEP program will find that these new dramatic scenes (both audio and video) provide more variety in their style of presentation. At times, the tapes illustrate typical parenting issues and suggested responses. At other times, participants respond to brief, open-ended scenes intended to stimulate discussion and role-play.

The original audiocassettes also included taped discussion of the practice situations from *The Parent's Handbook.* These practice situations are now included as separate exercises within the session plans.

7. Problem Situations. Each Problem Situation presents a brief, unfinished description of a typical conflict in a family. Have the members read the situation in *The Parent's Handbook* and discuss how they would answer the questions posed. There is no single correct answer; the situations permit members to apply the STEP principles and their new skills to the situation. If time permits, volunteers may role-play the situation and present ways to resolve the problem satisfactorily.

8. Summary. This is an essential part of the STEP program. Because a summary is held at the close of each meeting and each member is expected to contribute to the summary, participants become more conscious of what they are learning during the meeting.

The summary helps each member identify and clarify what she or he is learning. It also gives the leader feedback on what individual members and the group as a whole are learning. Misunderstandings and misinterpretations can be immediately corrected. There is an opportunity for instant feedback and clarification. The summaries can also give the leader some indication of participants' reactions to the way in which sessions are being conducted.

Summaries are invited by going around the group and asking, "What did you learn from this meeting?" or "What do you think about the ideas presented in this session?"

9. Activity for the Week. Each week, members are assigned a designated activity for the coming week. The assignment is designed to help parents internalize and put into action the STEP concepts learned in the session. Be sure the members understand their task, and indicate that at the next session they will have the opportunity to discuss their experiences.

10. Points to Remember. These are lists of the basic principles taught in each session. The principles have been presented on a single page in *The Parent's Handbook* which can be removed and posted as a reminder of essential steps for effective parenting. The page usually does not require further discussion, since the concepts have already been covered in the readings and tapes. Members should be encouraged to post the list in a prominent place at home to remind them of their new commitment.

11. My Plan for Improving Relationships. The plan for improving relationships permits participants to assess their own progress privately; the plan is not for discussion with the group. Each member identifies one or two major concerns and his or her typical response to these problems. The member decides which STEP principles might improve the relationship. The person then indicates what he or she plans to do as a result of what has been learned in the program. This procedure gives each member a chance to assess and record personal progress. The writing becomes a commitment to action, inviting further involvement.

12. Reading Assignment. To close the session, assign the designated chapter of *The Parent's Handbook* for the next session and explain its purpose.

Leading the STEP Study Group

You have agreed to lead a parent study group, but now some doubts may be setting in. You may be wondering:

- "Who do I think I am, telling other people how to raise their children?"
- "What if they ask me questions I can't answer? What do I do then?"
- "How can I get them to read the material and become involved with each other?"

Some anxiety is to be expected. It can be counteracted by a positive attitude and thoughtful preparation.

Setting the Tone

Make clear to the members of your group that you are not an authority on human behavior. Explain to the members that your job is to organize the group, present the program for each meeting, make the materials available, and lead the discussions so that all group members can participate profitably.

Of course you must prepare for each meeting by reading the *Leader's Manual* and *The Parent's Handbook*. It also helps to do some extra reading on the subject of raising children. (See "References for Further Study" at the end of Part One of this manual.) But most important will be your ability to communicate—to help make the subject of each meeting meaningful to group members.

Shelves of books have been written on the subject of people helping other people. One discovery that has come from all this is that effective group leaders need not be authorities on the subject of "helping." Far more pertinent are their abilities to listen well and to facilitate communication among group members. If you believe that it's more important to be an effective listener and facilitator than it is to have a precisely correct answer, you will realize that you need not be competent in all aspects of child training in order to respond to questions.

Answering Questions

A question comes up. It's directed to the leader. What do you do?

First, get other group members to think about the question. To the group, say something such as, "What do you think about that? How would you have handled that?" By doing so, you will tap the wisdom of the group and "universalize" the problem posed by the question. If the group cannot be mobilized, again redirect the question: "How would the authors of our program respond to that?"

Redirecting a question not only stimulates, involves, and brings the group together, it also demonstrates a leader's faith and belief in people's ability to find their own answers.

In "Florida Studies in the Helping Professions,"* Arthur Combs reports an extensive study of people who are in the business of helping other people. The

---

* University of Florida Social Science Monograph, No. 37, University of Florida Press, Gainesville, 1969.

difference between effective and ineffective helpers, he discovered, lay in their basic beliefs about people. The effective helpers believed that people are:

- *able,* not unable. They have the capacity to solve their problems.
- *friendly,* not unfriendly. They expect a reciprocal relationship.
- *worthy,* not unworthy. They possess dignity, which must be respected.
- basically *internally,* not *externally,* motivated. They are creative and motivated from within.
- *dependable,* not undependable. They are essentially trustworthy, predictable, and understandable.
- *helpful,* not hindering. They are sources of satisfaction and enhancement.

Results of the study indicate that a leader must genuinely hold these beliefs about people if the leader expects to encourage psychological growth. It is impossible to "sell" a democratic approach if one is authoritative and displays a lack of trust or acceptance in group meetings.

An effective leader must also project an impression of self-confidence. This rests upon a belief that one is adequate to meet the responsibilities and challenges of life. It comes from knowing that one is acceptable, likable, and able to bring about a positive response from people. A feeling of personal adequacy allows one to feel that sense of self-esteem which comes from being identified with others rather than alienated from them.

A feeling of personal adequacy also gives a leader something else—the courage to be imperfect. In the STEP program you do not have to be more competent than everyone else in the group. Nor do you have to feel that you must handle each situation perfectly. Because you believe in yourself, you are free to believe in others and in the power of the group.

Principles of Leadership

Leaders bring their personal beliefs and values to the group. Effective group leaders conduct each STEP session according to the following principles:

- Leaders accept a theory of human motivation that enables them to explain behavior in terms of its goal-directed nature.
- Leaders are sensitive to the potentially encouraging forces in a group and lead the group in a way which promotes cooperation and cohesiveness.
- Leaders believe in the ability of people to grow and change. Leaders are not involved in gratifying themselves, but in encouraging the growth of group members.
- Leaders provide experiences that allow group members to recognize their own assets. They avoid the role of expert or authority.
- Leaders encourage members to practice with their families what they have learned in the study group.
- Leaders are concerned with developing an atmosphere of mutual trust and encouragement among group members. They emphasize things individual parents are doing correctly, and they show faith and optimism when things seem to be going wrong.

Effective leaders will not possess all these desirable traits—no one does. But they will not be discouraged by their imperfections, either. They will proceed as well as they can, alert to ways they can improve.

How to Lead a Group

Since all STEP discussions are conducted in a group, an effective leader conducts meetings in such a way that members feel they share common concerns. In an atmosphere of mutuality, group members feel accepted when they raise problems. They feel, too, a willingness to listen, empathize, and learn from other members of their group.

An effective leader recognizes that group members learn best from each other, particularly if the content relates to child-training procedures a member has used successfully. Through "spectator learning," a person can sometimes listen to another's solution to a similar problem and apply the concepts without having to discuss them.

Most participants become willing to consider new ideas when they can release feelings about their own experiences in raising children. The expectation that members will apply new ideas enhances the involvement and commitment of all members.

When the group wanders unproductively, ask, "What is happening in our group?" "What guidelines are we failing to consider?"

Eight Study Group Leader Skills

The following skills of leadership can help each discussion be productive:

1. Structuring sets the purpose and goals of the group and the procedures of the meetings.

The purpose of a STEP study group is to consider how principles of child behavior can be applied to specific situations. The study group does not have to become involved in extensive discussions of the beliefs and values of its members. Instead, the focus is on understanding basic principles and their application.

Structuring establishes limits on discussions and redirects participants when they wander from the group's goals. Structuring requires the leader to be continuously aware of what is happening and to determine whether it is within the purposes of the group. The leader who structures well senses when it is appropriate to permit latitude in discussions and when it is prudent to draw boundaries.

To prevent unnecessary confusion, the leader should obtain early consensus about the time and place of meetings and discuss materials to be used.

2. Universalizing is the process whereby a leader helps group members become aware that their questions and concerns are shared by others.

If the members are to work together and to feel concern for each other, they must learn to listen to each other and discover that their concerns are not unique, but are often common experiences.

Group cohesion is promoted by a simple strategy, the leader's asking what others think about a presented problem.

After hearing a question or a puzzled comment, you may ask, "Has anyone else wondered about that? Has anyone else had difficulty trying to . . . ?" As responses come forth, listeners recognize they are not isolated in their lack of knowledge or in their ineffectiveness in influencing children's behavior.

3. Linking is the identification of common elements. It is a skill that requires a leader to listen carefully to the questions and comments expressed in the group.

As thoughts and feelings are expressed, listen for themes which are similar—but which may not have been recognized as such by other group members. Linking clarifies communication by helping members see that they have similar feelings or beliefs. Point out similarities or differences—for example, "Arlene gets very discouraged when she tries to deal with Wilson's ineptness. She seems to be saying, 'What's the use?' Do you remember Luisa's son, Emilio, getting Luisa to do things for him? Do you see any similarity between the two problems?"

As the common elements in their problems are pointed out, interaction between the members is promoted. *Linking is an especially important technique in the early stages of a group or when members are not listening to each other.*

4. Feedback is the process whereby a person gets reactions from members of the group concerning what he or she has just said or done. Feedback enables a person to understand how she or he is being perceived by others.

To build effective working relationships, group members must provide honest and specific feedback to each other. For the feedback process to work, group members must overcome some social taboos against the expression of thoughts and feelings.

The effective leader recognizes the value of feedback, points out its function in the group, and shows how it works by "feeding back" information to group members and clarifying what has happened. Feedback is most effective when it focuses on "here and now" situations that give members insight into how they act as parents. Saying to a member, "Your tone of voice and the way you appear to talk down to others comes across to me as disrespectful—could it be that your children are picking this up too?" gives the person information about the messages he or she conveys. Feedback does not demand a change; it only shares an observation. It must be done in a spirit of mutual respect and caring. Any decision to change rests with the receiver.

5. Developing tentative hypotheses enables members to translate theory into practice by finding principles applicable to the behavior of their own children.

The STEP program assumes that all behavior—and misbehavior—is purposive. As questions about the application of this principle arise, the leader asks members to describe:

a. What, specifically, did the child do?
b. How did you feel when this was happening?
c. How did you respond to the misbehavior?
d. How did the child respond to your reaction?
e. What purpose did the child's misbehavior have for the child?

By taking parents through these steps, the leader encourages them to look for the purposes of behavior. It is important to encourage members to feel free to guess or use hunches. In time, members can come to recognize that the freedom to risk error and to be imperfect allows them to grow by accepting their own best efforts.

6. Focusing on the positive behavior of children and parents gives members encouragement and leads them to encourage each other.

Ask: "What do you look forward to when you are with . . . ?" Or, "What can this child be respected or valued for?" Although this may be a difficult task, helping members focus on the positive will improve their relationships with their children and their feelings about themselves.

Recognize attempts by group members to function more effectively as parents. This will encourage at least minimal progress. Encouragement is a necessary skill for a parent; therefore, it should be practiced in the group. Members should learn to ask each other, "What are some ways in which you can encourage your child?"

7. Task setting and obtaining commitments is the process whereby group members are helped to clarify tasks and to specify the time commitments they are willing to make. To progress beyond general discussion, individual members must establish tasks and make definite commitments.

Task setting involves two steps: helping a parent identify a problem, and then helping him or her develop a specific procedure for solving it. Obtain a commitment by having the parent state an intention to apply the new procedure for a week and to report results at the next meeting of the group.

The leader uses task setting and commitment to help each member focus clearly on what she or he wants to get from the study group. These procedures also align the goals of the individual with those of the group.

8. Summarizing helps members to understand ideas, procedures, and attitudes that have been expressed and to integrate what they have learned. The summary is verbal, not written, so all may benefit from the exchange.

A summary may deal with the content of the meeting, the feelings of members, or the level of their involvement. Group members can be asked to summarize at appropriate times. The leader needn't wait until the end of a session to help clarify how he or she and other group members see the group's progress.

At the end of a session, a summary may lead group members to become aware of important things they missed during the session. This type of learning often occurs when the leader invites each member to tell what she or he learned from the session. The simple question, "What did you learn this time?" enables the leader to clarify mistaken impressions and improves the leader's understanding of the group as a whole.

Guidelines for Discussion Leaders

STEP is a parent education program that focuses on learning principles of behavior and applying them to parent-child relationships. STEP is not merely open discussion, nor is it family therapy. The program is intensive and will teach the group members new ideas and skills that can improve their effectiveness as parents. STEP is paced to keep the group involved with the basic concepts and skills of the program. It does not focus on intensive discussion of individual problems.

The Discussion Guidelines Poster presents the STEP ground rules for effective communication. The guidelines are presented and explained at the first meeting.

As leader, your effectiveness will increase as you help members to follow these guidelines. You will be most effective if you refrain from presenting yourself as an authority and demonstrate a democratic approach in the group. Model the principles; do not just talk about them. It is most important to demonstrate encouragement and logical consequences. Any tendency to use disparaging remarks will hinder your application of the principles of the program.

As the group proceeds, ask yourself:

1. Are we operating within the purpose, structure, and time requirements of this program?

2. How can I universalize the concern just raised so that other members can see its similarity to their own situations? (If in doubt, ask a question such as, "Has anyone else had a similar concern?")

3. Is the group cohesive, and do the members really listen to each other? You may "link" by pointing out the similarity between two themes, or by asking, "How is this (question or situation) similar to something we've already discussed?" Linkage promotes cohesiveness as it enables the group to review program concepts.

4. Are the members of the group communicating so that each member is coming to know how she or he is experienced by others in the group? The group will learn to use feedback best if you, as leader, clearly describe what you are experiencing. If the group has developed trust, the feedback process can be accelerated at points by having a "go-'round" in which you express to each person how you as the leader experience him or her concerning a particular issue.

5. Are the members understanding the purposive nature of behavior, and can they develop hypotheses about the specific purposes of a child's "misbehavior"? This can be determined by asking, "For what purpose does the child do that?" When a parent is not sure how to determine purpose, help the person to reconsider the child's actions, their own feelings, and the consequences of their corrective efforts, as each gives a clue to the child's motivation.

6. Are the members learning how to use encouragement? If they are not, focus more strongly on assets: "What is _____'s strongest trait for dealing with this situation? What are some other strengths we see in _____?"

7. Are group members applying the concepts and making commitments to acquire the skills the program offers? If not, ask, "What could you do to learn more about that principle and how it applies to your child?" (Perhaps rereading the appropriate chapter in *The Parent's Handbook* should be suggested.)

8. Are members spending too much time on one issue, or starting to debate and intellectualize? If so, you can summarize, "It seems that some group members feel _____, while others believe _____. Let's limit discussion to three more minutes. Then we will have to go on to the next question." And do go on.

9. Is a member making a suggestion that seems inappropriate? To get the person to consider the implications of what is being said, ask, "What might happen if that is done?"

10. Are the members talking only to the leader, rather than to each other? You might say, "Would you please tell Mrs. Smith directly, with an I-message, how you feel?"

11. What are the members learning? One of the most important experiences in the course is the summary. Summaries can be held at any point in a session, but the leader should take care to end each session by asking each participant, "What did you learn during this meeting?" Members may talk about themselves or about a principle. The summary process will help each person focus on personal experience and will help the leader determine how the group as a whole is understanding and applying the material.

12. You may be asked questions that invite you to answer "right" or "wrong." At such times, clarify the ground rules of communication—to discuss and apply, not to debate. State what you believe, and emphasize that others can believe what they choose. Avoid getting into a power struggle with the person asking the question.

Keeping a Group Going

Experienced leaders have found that parent study groups tend to move through three stages:

In the *first stage,* the group shows enthusiasm and unrealistic expectations. Members assume that the group meetings will solve all their child-raising problems. They place high expectations on the leader. Some will try to manipulate the leader into the role of authority. This may be initially flattering, but you should avoid it. If you do not, members will soon become disenchanted; you cannot live up to their expectations. What the dependent or manipulative group members want is to avoid responsibility. What they must learn instead is that to become effective parents, they must assume responsibility for changing themselves; they cannot expect you, or some magical remedy, to do it for them.

During this initial phase, some members may feel anxious, fearful, and distrustful about disclosing their parent-child concerns. If all group members do not know each other well, some may feel socially isolated.

In this early phase, leaders can reduce some of the group's tenseness with appropriate humor and a relaxed attitude. You can help relax the group also by describing common difficulties of child-rearing and suggesting that these problems are probably experienced by most members of the group.

In the *second stage,* members' commitment and enthusiasm may lessen. This usually occurs when they recognize that they are the ones who must change if their children are to change. At this point, expect some discouragement expressed as negative opinions about the value of the group.

During this second phase, you must continually redefine goals, facilitate feedback, encourage efforts and progress, and use techniques such as role-playing to increase members' interest.

In the *third stage,* members are generally on task. The group has matured to the point of assuming responsibility for its own learning. As members become a cohesive unit, they become more effective in teaching each other.

Problems of Group Leadership

Even experienced group leaders encounter difficulties. Many of these problems can be traced to a common denominator: the participant who resists—knowingly *or unknowingly*—what the rest of the group is trying to accomplish.

Communicating honestly and directly is not easy. Accepting new ideas is no simple matter either. When we feel unsure of ourselves, we may defend ourselves by "playing games." To help you identify the use of these ploys, we have classified manipulative behavior in terms of games:

1. Monopoly. People who play "Monopoly" believe they must be the center of attention. They become concerned whenever they are not the focus of discussion. These people have a number of purposes for monopolizing a group. Aside from enjoying the attention of other members, they develop strategies for controlling and contesting the position of the leader.

To lessen the influence of a monopolizer, you might say, "I'm getting concerned that time is going fast and we need to move on to other things. If there's time later, we can come back to this." Then move on.

If the individual is not influenced by feedback from the group, meet with the person after the meeting to deal directly with the issue. At that time, send an I-message about the member's behavior: "When you keep us busy with you, I can't help group members get involved with the material and with each other."

If the member continues trying to monopolize the group, ask him or her to drop membership. Suggest that the person consider individual parent counseling, where more time can be given.

2. Prove It. People who play this game challenge the leader, other members, the material, and anything else which to them symbolizes authority. They challenge in order to reveal the fallibility of the resources, to set themselves up as particularly intelligent, or to assume the leadership role.

A leader needs to identify the purpose of this behavior and the beliefs that motivate it. If a member who plays this game is challenging mainly to be the center of discussion (if the person believes "I count only if other people are involved with me"), you need to find a way to encourage the person by recognizing assets and contributions. However, if the member is concerned with power and gaining a role of authority, you may need group assistance to redirect the person. Try asking the group, "What seems to be happening in the group now?" or, "How do you feel about what Joan is saying?" This will usually bring about a solution. If members offer feedback to the challenger and you move on to the next phase of the lesson, the problem is usually resolved.

If the person does not understand the confrontation of other members, review the Discussion Guidelines Poster and clarify the meaning of effective communication. You might say, "These ideas are for all of us to consider and to make our own decisions on whether or not to accept them." In whatever course you choose, be sure to avoid a struggle for power.

3. Yakkity-Yak. Group members who talk incessantly may do so for recognition or because they believe their problems are more important than those of other group members. You can sometimes redirect chatterboxes by recognizing their enthusiasm and privately asking them to encourage more reserved members of the group to become involved in the discussion. To move the talker from chattering to putting principles into action, suggest that she or he apply a very specific principle for the following week.

People whose talk in the group focuses only on themselves may be redirected with the question, "How does what you're saying relate to the concerns expressed by _____?" or "Could we go on and come back to this later if there's time?"

4. Try to Make Me. Group members who play this game have only a partial commitment to the program. Their motivation is superficial—they want something to give them magical control over their children. When the leader points out that they must be responsible for their own results, they show resistance.

In some instances, the program's ideas may conflict with a resister's basic beliefs. If such a parent believes that any questioning of his or her practices is a personal challenge, he or she will fight at every turn—either actively or passively.

To a resister, you can say, "We cannot tell you what to do; you must decide what's best for yourself. Our purpose is to study the ideas set forth in this program, so we need to continue." Taking this stance, you imply that the resister is entitled to his or her beliefs, but not entitled to disrupt the purpose of the group.

If resisters can come to see that their personal opinions are not being threatened from the outside, they may eventually become more cooperative. In any event, by remaining objective you have demonstrated a way to deal with the invitation to a power struggle.

5. Have You Considered . . . Let's Look at All Points of View.
Intellectualizers are similar to those who play "Try to Make Me." They resist
with ideas, rather than with emotions. When the group is moving along, they
enjoy interrupting its progress by bringing in a different point of view—often
seemingly important.

You can indicate that the person may have a point, but that the group is organized
to consider and discuss the opinions and ideas presented in the program. Clarify
that the leader's task is to help the group focus on what the program has to offer.

6. I'll Try It. One of the requirements of the STEP program is that parents
make consistent, firm commitments. If some parents begin to move toward
action by stating, "I like the idea of (for example, logical consequences for
chores); I may try it," you need to use the "shock approach" and ask them firmly
not to try it. Indicate that the word "try" implies a mere attempt, and if they fail,
they can say, "Well, I tried." Ask them to either change nothing, or *commit*
themselves to following a new course of action at least until the next session.
Emphasize that one must begin a new approach with a firm decision. Remind
them that expectations have much to do with success and failure.

7. Kids Will Do That . . . It's Only Normal . . . It's Just a Stage. One of
the most common deterrents to group progress is the acceptance of all kinds of
misbehavior and ineffective relationships as normal for parent-child relationships.
People who promote this view believe that children are unavoidably "impossible
to live with," hence only to be endured. They see no hope of helping children
become cooperative, responsible, and enjoyable.

If such a parent contributes very many gloomy pronouncements ("That's how
kids are . . ."), you must block the attempts to reduce the group to futility.
Confront their beliefs by stating, "You may feel it's impossible to improve
relationships, but that has not been the experience of others. We are here because
we believe we *can* change behavior and improve our relationships with
children." Do not argue.

8. If Only He or She Would. Some parents shift the responsibility for
unsatisfactory parent-child relationships to a spouse, grandparent, neighbor, or
some other person. In effect, such a parent is saying that a child's misbehavior
is not influenced by the parent's own behavior, that someone else must act if
things are to improve. When a leader reflects a position in the extreme ("You
seem to be saying that nothing you say or do has any bearing on the relationship
with your child"), the speaker can become aware of what he or she is really
saying.

If this is ineffective, state that this program is to clarify what each individual
can do, not what others should do. "We assume responsibility for our own
behavior. Then we are free to decide what to do about it."

9. What Do You Do When . . . ? The group will be likely to have a
"catastrophizer," one who enjoys narrating details of calamities. This person
tends to present very difficult problems and then resist suggestions for solutions,
by pointing out, "But what if . . . ?" The member who plays "What do you
do when . . . ?" usually has not experienced the object of his or her concern
firsthand.

The leader can ask, "Are you aware that when you say, 'What if . . . ?' it seems to me you are looking for reasons not to change what you're presently doing?"

The leader can also turn the resister's question around by asking, "When the child did that, how did *you* respond?" Such redirection enables the group to look again at the purpose or consequence of the behavior. Continue by asking, "What principle did you overlook?" "Which principle could apply?" Do not permit the individuals to continue generalizing and intellectualizing. Require them to be specific.

Alternately the leader can respond, "Of course anything can happen; but let's work from our own concrete experiences."

10. Yes, But . . . Members who play this game are communicating to the rest of the group that they have no intention of accepting new ideas or making commitments. By saying, "Yes, but . . . ," or words to that effect, they intend only to impress the group with their good intentions. They dare not risk stating yes or no.

The leader can confront vague or vacillating members with encouragement: "When you say, 'Yes, but . . . ,' it sounds as if you're talking about something you really don't want to do. That's all right. It's not the purpose of this program to pressure you to do anything you don't want to do."

Or, refer the problem to the group: "What is George really saying?" If the group does not understand the meaning of George's message, express your own impressions.

The foregoing games occur because people are being asked to change before they have new skills and attitudes to replace the games. Through respect and patience, the leader can help parents learn more honest ways to express themselves in the group as well as with their children.

Understanding the Child

What does a leader need to know about human behavior to conduct a STEP parent study group?

You do not have to be a specialist in child psychology, but you do need to understand the presented principles of human behavior, particularly as they apply to children.

This section will set forth the principles used in the STEP program. Read them carefully. They are the foundation for most of the material in the program.

The Purposes of Behavior*

Human behavior can be better explained in terms of its pattern and purpose than in terms of cause and effect.

To understand a person's current behavior, do not seek answers from descriptions of the past. Instead, look for the purpose that person's behavior serves. The behavior is not random or meaningless. It points toward and achieves

---

*More information about the purposes, or goals, of behavior can be found in *The Parent's Handbook.*

something for the person; it brings about a certain benefit. Find the purpose—the goal, or the benefit—and you will understand why she or he is behaving a certain way.

For example: Some people search for "causes" of low achievement by a child of high ability. We do not look for causes. We look instead for purposes—how the behavior (in this instance, the low achievement) serves the person who exhibits it. In the foregoing example, it makes sense to the child to underachieve. Doing so may bring special control and power over those people—teachers or parents—who want the child to do better. Or, it may simply bring special attention from teachers and parents. Underachievement may serve to excuse the child from functioning or may be used to "get even" with the parents. Knowing that underachievement serves a purpose—what the child gains by attaining low grades—enables us to understand and help change behavior.

To repeat: the STEP program starts from the viewpoint that *all behavior is purposive*. Behavior is directed toward some goal—toward achieving something for the person, even though the person is probably not aware of the goal of his or her own behavior. The goal offers the proper explanation for behavior. Do not search in the past for causes; try to identify what the behavior achieves for a person.

The goals of misbehavior in children were first described by Rudolf Dreikurs, an eminent psychiatrist who was associated with the Alfred Adler Institute of Chicago. Dreikurs believed that a child misbehaves to achieve one of the following goals or purposes:

- Attention
- Power
- Revenge
- Display of inadequacy

Parents can recognize which goal their child's behavior is serving by two simple methods:

1. By becoming aware of what they feel when the child misbehaves, and
2. By observing how the child responds to their attempts at correction.

Children whose goal is *attention* believe they can find their place only by having others pay attention to them. They may gain attention by acting cute, trying to impress or charm, or being nuisances or pests. You can recognize this goal when you feel annoyed and impatient. When you correct them, they stop the misbehavior temporarily—that is, they have achieved their goal. Later they may repeat the misbehavior or do something else for attention.

Children whose goal is *power* want to be boss and have their own way. They may be openly disobedient, defiant of authority, or stubborn; or, they may show passive resistance—proving you can't make them do anything. You can recognize this goal when you feel anger and a desire to establish or regain control. The children will defy you, either actively or passively, by continuing to misbehave. Or, they will stop temporarily and then intensify their actions. Or, they will do as they are told, but not to your satisfaction.

Children whose goal is *revenge* may be violent or sullen in their defiance. These are the children who want to get even; they want to strike back. In response, you feel hurt, resentful, and outraged. You try to get even and the children respond by seeking further revenge.

Children whose goal is to *display inadequacy* act as if they are stupid, inept, or inferior. They believe they are hopeless and want to show that they can't be counted on. You recognize this goal when you feel confused and helpless and believe there is nothing more that can be done. The children respond passively or fail to respond. No improvement is seen, although you feel as if you have "done everything." The situation may seem hopeless.

Family Constellation

It is important, too, that parents understand the influence of the family constellation on the development of children. Each child has a different position in the family and therefore perceives all family events from a viewpoint different from all others. Consequent competition between children strengthens basic differences in personality: where one child succeeds, the other may tend to fail; where one child feels encouraged to go ahead with his or her talents, the other may feel discouraged and tend to withdraw.

In studying the family constellation, we should note the ordinal positions of children: oldest, second, middle, youngest, or only child. These positions have their own characteristic lines of development and, as a result, their own characteristic beliefs and attitudes. However, we should not encourage parents to think of their children only in terms of ordinal position. It is more important for parents to try to understand the related *psychological position* of each child—that is, to understand how the child interprets his or her own situation as it relates to the family constellation. Some oldest children, for example, do not hold off the challenge to their position by younger siblings. The youngest child sometimes refuses to be the baby and strives instead to be first.

Certainly the sex and ages of brothers and sisters and the attitudes of parents influence each child's attitudes toward life. If a boy is born after a number of girls, or if the oldest child is a girl in a family that values boys, the child's psychological position is influenced and, in turn, influences the person's outlook on life.

The characteristic ordinal positions of children in a family are as follows:

First-born children have a place before other children arrive. They receive considerable attention before they are suddenly dethroned. They want to continue to be first, and so they strive to protect their favored position. In activities in which they cannot maintain supremacy, first-born children may lose interest. Some become very discouraged and "best" at exhibiting uncooperative behavior.

Second children are confronted with someone who is always ahead of them. They may either feel inadequate, because older children can do things which they cannot, or feel they have to catch up by striving to become what the older child is not. Second children may, for example, become more aggressive or more passive, more dependent or more self-sufficient.

Middle children frequently feel squeezed out, deprived of the rights and privileges awarded the eldest and the baby. They may come to believe life is unfair, or they may decide to overcome the disadvantages of their position by elevating themselves above their older siblings.

Youngest children are the "babies" of the family. They appear to have fewer rights, and so they may find their place by being the cutest, weakest, or most inept. They may demand service or become little tyrants.

Only children experience their formative years among people who are bigger and more capable. They tend to develop a style that ensures a place among adults. They may become verbal, charming, intelligent, or—if it suits their purpose—shy and helpless. Often they expect to have their own way.

The Way We Seek to Be Known

Another behavioral principle underlying the STEP program is this: We present ourselves to others in a manner which we intend will portray our beliefs about ourselves. Some of us, for example, try to be known as more competent than others. Some of us prefer to be known as socially inferior and intellectually deficient, so that nothing is expected of us.

All Behavior Has Social Meaning

Thus, to analyze behavior, we ask: "How does this behavior help the person present the image he or she wants to convey?"

All human behavior has social meaning. People's behavior reflects how they interpret the world and how they see themselves in it, particularly in relation to others.

People's behavior usually makes sense in a social context. Thus, to understand behavior, look for its social consequences—how other people respond. For example: When Kara misbehaves, she is doing so to achieve an expected response. Maybe she knows Dad will clean her room for her if she does a poor job.

An important assumption in the STEP program is that all people—both children and adults—are decision-making, self-determining beings. People are *not* victims of fate or heredity. They make choices based on how they interpret the world. People's choices always fit their purposes—even though they may not be totally aware of their purposes.

An effective group leader knows that one must understand people's private logic (how they interpret their experiences) before one can understand their behavior.

References for Further Study

Below is a list of references to help you learn more about the philosophies and skills taught in STEP. Another source of further information is the North American Society of Adlerian Psychology, a very active group devoted to spreading Adlerian and related materials. Membership is open to anyone interested in Adlerian psychology. To find out more about this society, write North American Society of Adlerian Psychology, 159 North Dearborn, Chicago, IL 60601.

Booklets
The following booklets can be ordered from CMTI Press, Box 8268, Coral Springs, FL 33065:

The Basics Series
Carlson, Jon. *Basics of Discipline.* Coral Springs, Fla.: CMTI Press, 1978.

_____. *Basics of Stress Management.* Coral Springs, Fla.: CMTI Press, 1982.

Dinkmeyer, Don. *Basics of Adult-Teen Relationships.* Coral Springs, Fla.: CMTI Press, 1976.

_____. *Basics of Self-Acceptance.* Coral Springs, Fla.: CMTI Press, 1977.

Dinkmeyer, Don, Jr., and James S. Dinkmeyer. *Basics of Parenting.* Coral Springs, Fla.: CMTI Press, 1980.

McKay, Gary D. *Basics of Encouragement.* Coral Springs, Fla.: CMTI Press, 1976.

Audiocassettes

Dinkmeyer, Don, and Gary D. McKay. *Raising a Responsible Child.* Waco, Tex.: Success Motivation Cassettes, 1983.

The following audiocassettes can be ordered from CMTI Press, Box 8268, Coral Springs, FL 33065:

Carlson, Jon. *Stress Management for Children and Adults.* Coral Springs, Fla.: CMTI Press, 1982.

Dinkmeyer, Don. *Encouragement: Becoming a Positive Person.* Coral Springs, Fla.: CMTI Press, 1982.

Dinkmeyer, Don, and Gary D. McKay. *Discipline.* Coral Springs, Fla.: CMTI Press, 1982.

_____. *STEP Parent Education.* Coral Springs, Fla.: CMTI Press, 1982.

Kern, Roy. *Lifestyle Interpretation.* Coral Springs, Fla.: CMTI Press, 1982.

McKay, Gary D. *Self-Confidence: How to Get It and How to Keep It.* Coral Springs, Fla.: CMTI Press, 1982.

Books

Ackerman, Robert J. *Children of Alcoholics.* 2d ed. Homes Beach, Fla.: Learning Publications, 1983.

Adler, Alfred. *Understanding Human Nature.* London: Unwin, 1918; Greenwich, Conn.: Premier Books, 1957.

Allred, Hugh. *Mission for Mother.* Salt Lake City, Utah: Bookcraft, 1968.

Ansbacher, Heinz L., and Rowena R. Ansbacher, eds. *The Individual Psychology of Alfred Adler.* New York: Harper and Row, 1956.

Atlas, Stephen L. *Parents Without Partners.* Philadelphia: Running Press, 1984.

Baruth, Leroy G. *A Single Parent's Survival Guide: How to Raise the Children.* Dubuque, Iowa: Kendall/Hunt, 1979.

Benson, Herbert. *Beyond the Relaxation Response.* New York: Times Books, 1984.

Branden, Nathaniel. *The Psychology of Self-Esteem.* New York: Bantam, 1969.

Briggs, Dorothy Corkille. *Your Child's Self-Esteem.* New York: Dolphin Books, 1975.

Christensen, Oscar C., and Thomas G. Schramski, eds. *Adlerian Family Counseling.* Minneapolis: Educational Media Corporation, 1983.

Currier, C. *Learning to Step Together.* Baltimore: Stepfamily Association of America, 1982.

Danziger, Sanford, and Rivka B. Danziger. *You Are Your Own Best Counselor.* Honolulu: Self-Mastery Systems, 1984.

Dewey, Edith. *Basic Applications of Adlerian Psychology.* Coral Springs, Fla.: CMTI Press, 1978.

Dilly, Josiah. *And I Thought I Knew How to Communicate.* Minneapolis: Educational Media Corporation, 1985.

Dinkmeyer, Don. "Developing Personal Accountability Through Natural and Logical Consequences." In *Experts Advise Parents,* edited by E. Schiff, 173-99. New York: Dell, 1987.

Dinkmeyer, Don, and Rudolf Dreikurs. *Encouraging Children to Learn: The Encouragement Process.* New York: Elsevier-Dutton, 1979.

Dinkmeyer, Don, and Lewis Losoncy. *The Encouragement Book: Becoming a Positive Person.* Englewood Cliffs, N.J.: Prentice-Hall, 1980.

Dinkmeyer, Don, and Gary D. McKay. *Raising a Responsible Child: Practical Steps to Successful Family Relationships.* New York: Simon and Schuster, 1973.

Dinkmeyer, Don, Don Dinkmeyer, Jr., and Len Sperry. *Adlerian Counseling and Psychotherapy.* 2d ed. Columbus, Ohio: Merrill, 1987.

Dinkmeyer, Don, Gary D. McKay, and Joyce L. McKay. *New Beginnings: Parent's Manual*. Champaign, Ill.: Research Press, 1987.

Dreikurs, Rudolf. *The Challenge of Parenthood*. New York: Duell, Sloan, Pearce, 1948.

_____. *Fundamentals of Adlerian Psychology*. New York: Greenberg, 1950.

_____. *Psychodynamics, Psychotherapy and Counseling: Collected Papers*. Chicago: Alfred Adler Institute, 1967.

Dreikurs, Rudolf, and Loren Grey. *Logical Consequences: A New Approach to Discipline*. New York: Meredith Press, 1968.

Dreikurs, Rudolf, and Vicki Soltz. *Children: The Challenge*. New York: Hawthorn, 1964.

Einstein, Elizabeth. *The Stepfamily: Living, Loving, and Learning*. New York: Macmillan, 1982.

Einstein, Elizabeth, and Linda Albert. *Stepfamily Living: Pitfalls and Possibilities*. Tampa, Fla.: Einstein and Albert, 1983.

Elkind, David. *The Hurried Child*. Reading, Mass.: Addison-Wesley, 1981.

_____. *Miseducation: Preschoolers at Risk*. New York: Alfred Knopf, 1987.

Ellis, Albert. *How to Live with and without Anger*. New York: Reader's Digest Press, 1977.

_____. *Reason and Emotion in Psychotherapy*. Hollywood, Calif. and Secaucus, N.J.: Citadel, 1977.

Ellis, Albert, and Robert A. Harper. *A New Guide to Rational Living*. North Hollywood, Calif.: Wilshire Books, 1975.

Ellis, Albert, Janet L. Wolfe, and Sandra Mosely. *How to Raise an Emotionally Healthy, Happy Child*. North Hollywood, Calif.: Wilshire Books, 1972.

Glenn, H. Stephen, and Jane Nelsen. *Raising Children for Success*. Fair Oaks, Calif.: Sunrise, 1987.

Gordon, Thomas. *Parent Effectiveness Training*. New York: Peter H. Wyden, 1970.

Hauck, Paul. *The Rational Management of Children*. Roslyn Heights, N.Y.: Libra Publishers, 1972.

Jacobson, Edmund. *You Must Relax*. New York: McGraw-Hill, 1957.

King, Linda. *Mine, Yours or Still Ours?* Maple Ridge, British Columbia: Maple Ridge Family Education Centre, 1983.

Maultsby, Maxie C. *Help Yourself to Happiness Through Rational Self-Counseling*. New York: Institute for Rational Living, 1975.

Meyer, Roberta. *The Parent Connection: How to Communicate with Your Child about Alcohol and Other Drugs*. London: Franklin Watts, 1984.

Milgram, Gail Gleason. *What, When and How to Talk to Children about Alcohol and Other Drugs: A Guide for Parents*. Center City, Minn.: Hazelden Foundation, 1983.

Mosak, Harold H. *On Purpose*. Chicago: Alfred Adler Institute, 1977.

Nelsen, Jane. *Positive Discipline*. Fair Oaks, Calif.: Sunrise, 1981.

Paris, Erna. *Stepfamilies: Making Them Work*. New York: Avon Books, 1985.

Perkins, William Mack, and Nancy McMurtrie-Perkins. *Raising Drug-Free Kids in a Drug-Filled World*. Center City, Minn.: Hazelden Foundation, 1986.

Schnebly, Lee. *Out of Apples*. Tucson: Manzanas Press, 1984.

Sherman, Robert, and Don Dinkmeyer. *Systems of Family Therapy: An Adlerian Integration*. New York: Brunner/Mazel, 1987.

Tubesing, Donald A. *Kicking Your Stress Habits*. New York: New American Library, Signet Books, 1981.

Tubesing, Nancy Loving, and Donald A. Tubesing. *Structured Exercises in Stress Management*. Duluth, Minn.: Whole Person Press, 1986.

Visher, Emily B., and John S. Visher. *How to Win as a Stepfamily*. New York: Dembner, 1982.

_____. *Stepfamilies: A Guide to Working with Stepparents and Stepchildren*. New York: Brunner/Mazel, 1979.

Walker, Glynnis. *Second Wife, Second Best?* New York: Doubleday, 1984.

Wegscheider, Sharon. *Another Chance*. Palo Alto: Science and Behavior Books, 1981.

Woititz, Janet G. *Adult Children of Alcoholics*. Pompano Beach, Fla.: Health Communications, Inc., 1983.

Youngs, Bette B. *Stress in Children*. New York: Avon Books, 1985.

Yura, Michael T., and Lawrence Zuckerman. *Raising the Exceptional Child: Meeting the Everyday Challenges of the Handicapped or Retarded Child*. New York: Hawthorn, 1979.

Journal Articles
Brassington, Robert. "The Changing Family Constellation in Single Parent Families." *Individual Psychology* 38, no. 4 (1982): 369-78.

Martin, Maggie, and Don Martin. "Counseling the Child of Divorce: Emphasizing the Positive Aspects." *Individual Psychology* 39, no. 2 (1983): 180-85.

Teaching Programs

Dinkmeyer, Don, and Jon Carlson. *Time for a Better Marriage*. Circle Pines, Minn.: American Guidance Service, 1984.

Dinkmeyer, Don, and Gary D. McKay. *Systematic Training for Effective Parenting of Teens*. Circle Pines, Minn.: American Guidance Service, 1983.

Dinkmeyer, Don, Gary D. McKay, and Don Dinkmeyer, Jr. *Systematic Training for Effective Teaching*. Circle Pines, Minn.: American Guidance Service, 1980.

Dinkmeyer, Don, Gary D. McKay, and Joyce L. McKay. *New Beginnings: Skills for Single Parents and Stepfamily Parents*. Champaign, Ill.: Research Press, 1987.

Dinkmeyer, Don, Gary D. McKay, Don Dinkmeyer, Jr., James S. Dinkmeyer, and Joyce L. McKay. *The Next STEP: Effective Parenting Through Problem Solving*. Circle Pines, Minn.: American Guidance Service, 1987.

Soltz, Vicki. *Study Group Leader's Manual*. Chicago: Alfred Adler Institute, 1967. (To be used with *Children: The Challenge*.)

Sweeney, Thomas. *A Study Guide for Education: Coping with Kids*. Athens, Ohio: Ohio University Press Extension Division, 1977.

Part Two
Sessions

Understanding Children's Behavior and Misbehavior

Materials

- *The Parent's Handbook:* Chapter 1, "Understanding Children's Behavior and Misbehavior"
- Videocassette 1 *or* Audiocassette 1, Side B: "The Four Goals of Misbehavior"
- *Script Booklet:* Session 1 Tapescript
- Discussion Guidelines Poster
- Chart 1A: The Goals of Misbehavior
- Chart 1B: The Goals of Positive Behavior

Objectives

This lesson has three purposes: orienting the group to the method of study that will be used in the program; getting group members acquainted with each other; and introducing members to a practical theory for understanding their children.

In this session, parents will learn that their children's misbehavior serves one general purpose: to assure themselves that they have a place in the family. Parents will also learn how to identify their children's mistaken goals. Finally, they will learn how parents unintentionally reinforce their children's misbehavior.

Procedures

1. Introduction

Begin the first session by introducing yourself and stating the objectives of the program. Say:

In the STEP program, you will

- **Learn a practical theory of human behavior.**
- **Learn ways to establish more effective relationships with your children.**
- **Learn how to use encouragement.**
- **Develop skills for listening, resolving conflicts, and exploring alternatives with your children.**
- **Improve communication between yourself and your children.**
- **Learn an approach to discipline called "natural and logical consequences."**
- **Learn how to conduct effective family meetings.**

Invite members to become acquainted with each other by asking each person to give his or her name and the names and ages of the children, beginning with the oldest child. Have each member repeat the name of every other person in the group so that everyone can become acquainted on a first-name basis. You might say: **In order to become better acquainted, repeat the first name of each person in the group introduced before you. Then give your own name and the names and ages of your children, beginning with the oldest child.**

Take a survey of the group. Ask what the members expect to get from the meetings by saying: **People come to parent study groups for various reasons. What do you hope to get from this experience?** Then clarify your role by telling the group that you are here to facilitate discussion of the materials presented in the program, not to give detailed advice on individual child-training questions. Emphasize that through learning the principles they will be able to relate more effectively to their children. Point out that you are not here as an authority. As the meeting goes on, remind members that parent study groups are for the purposes of discussion and skill development. If there are mistaken impressions, briefly clarify what the STEP program offers.

From the beginning, it is important to establish a democratic style of leadership. Encourage all to participate and point out the disadvantages of monologues and dialogues.

Explain the Discussion Guidelines Poster. Say: **So that all may benefit from the program, here are some discussion guidelines to assist our communication with each other. This poster will be displayed at each meeting so we can keep the principles in mind as we proceed with our discussions.**

Point to each guideline and explain it briefly using wording similar to the following:

1. **Stay on the topic.** It is easy to wander, generalize, and drift into social conversation. At every point in the discussion we should be checking to see whether we are on the topic or avoiding the task. When we are not sure, we can ask ourselves, "How does this relate to what we are discussing?"

2. **Become involved in the discussion.** We will benefit most when all members of the group are thinking about a common concern and sharing their thoughts. If you are confused or do not understand something, ask a question. If you see another side to an issue, present it. We are here to understand the ideas presented in STEP and to decide how they will apply to our situation.

   If some members of the group are always silent, we may ask them, "What do you think about this?" It is your responsibility as a member of the group to express your thoughts and feelings about the material we are covering.

3. **Share the time.** We will learn most by sharing the time. If we sense that some of us are monopolizing the time, we can check by asking, "What seems to be keeping the group from making more progress?"

4. **Be patient—take one step at a time.** As you are exposed to new ideas, you will often have more questions than answers. You will also want to see instant change in your children and even in yourself. However, it is more reasonable to attempt one thing at a time than to attack several problems at once. We may ask, "Are you expecting too much of yourself and your children?"

5. **Encourage each other.** Encouragement is basic to producing change and helping people feel self-confident. We will seek to become more encouraging

by learning how to encourage each other. We may ask, "How can we encourage _____?" and "How can _____ encourage his or her child?" With practice, the skill should generalize to our relationships with children.

6. Be responsible for your own behavior. Each of us must take responsibility for his or her own actions and for making certain that comments and actions are constructive. A basic principle of this program is that each person is responsible for changing his or her own behavior. Parents must be willing to change if they expect their children to change. We will not let you excuse yourself by shifting responsibility onto your children, your spouse, or the situation. We will be asking, "What can you do to change your situation?"

Ask group members if they have questions about the Discussion Guidelines Poster, and then leave it on display.

2. Reading Assignment

If participants do not already have their copies of *The Parent's Handbook,* pass the handbooks out at this time. Have participants turn to Chapter 1, and allow from 10 to 15 minutes for them to read the chapter.

After parents have finished reading, use one of the following procedures to discuss the material. (Note: The leader's goal is to create an atmosphere that encourages open discussion. Your behavior in this session will establish expectations for ensuing sessions.)

Alternative A. You can begin an open discussion by asking, **What did you learn from this reading?** and **How would you apply these ideas?** or, **Do you have any questions about the reading?** This should initiate a discussion that follows the group's interests. Discussion should focus on:

1. What the ideas and principles mean, and

2. Ways to apply these ideas and principles.

Alternative B. If you prefer a more organized format, use the following questions. These questions are supplied as guidelines; they are not intended to limit discussion. Alter the wording to suit your own style.

1. The reading states that today's parents need training. What has happened in society to make this training necessary?

2. Why is reward and punishment as a method of discipline no longer as effective as it was in the past?

3. The authors suggest using democratic procedures with children as an alternative to the autocratic methods of reward and punishment. What do they mean by "democratic procedures"?

4. What do the authors believe about human behavior? How does this apply to children?

5. Why do children misbehave? What are the four goals of misbehavior?

6. What are two techniques you can use to discover the goal of your child's misbehavior? How do you know if your child is seeking the goal of attention?

Power? Revenge? Display of inadequacy? Why is it important to know what goal the child is seeking?

7. In general, what do the authors say we should do when our children inappropriately seek attention? When they seek power? When they seek revenge? When they display inadequacy?

8. Why do we need to concentrate on changing our own behavior rather than on changing the child's behavior?

9. What are the four basic ingredients for building a positive relationship?

3. Chart 1A: The Goals of Misbehavior

Take a few minutes to display and discuss Chart 1A, using wording similar to the following:

The first column on the left describes the child's faulty beliefs about himself or herself and about the way to gain a place in the family. The second column tells the goal the child pursues to support this faulty belief. The third and fourth columns describe the consequences of misbehavior that are related to each goal. The fifth column suggests alternatives.

The parent's typical responses in the third column give clues to the child's goal. For example, if your response is to feel annoyed and to remind and coax the child with the result that the child temporarily stops the misbehavior, the child's goal has been to receive attention.

The last column gives some general suggestions about how to stop reinforcing the child's goal and how to redirect the misbehavior.

Go over each example on the chart. Then ask: **Do you have any questions about the chart?**

4. Presentation of Tape

The taped segment for this session is on Videocassette 1 *or* Audiocassette 1, Side B. Turn in your *Script Booklet* to the tapescript for Session 1 and follow the directions for conducting the taped presentation and discussion.

5. Discussion of the Tape

At the end of the tape, a number of people may be ready to ask questions. The preferred method of discussion is to follow topics raised by group members. However, if members are not ready to ask questions, you can begin the discussion with an open question: **What do you think about the ideas on the tape?**

If the group needs more direction, consider these topics:

a. How to determine the goal of a child's misbehavior.

b. When you fight or when you give in, you are likely to increase the child's desire for power.

c. Retaliation invites further revenge.

d. Children who display inadequacy usually are not unable—rather, they lack *belief* in their ability.

e. Steps parents can instead take to begin to redirect misbehavior (see Chart 1A).

f. The positive counterparts of the four goals of misbehavior.

6. Chart 1B: The Goals of Positive Behavior

Take a few minutes to display and discuss Chart 1B, using wording similar to the following:

The first column on the left of this chart explains the child's positive beliefs about himself or herself and about how she or he can belong. The next column indicates the goal the child is seeking. The third column illustrates the type of positive behavior the child engages in to achieve the goal. The last column gives some general ideas for encouraging positive goals and behavior.

Go over each example on the chart. Then ask: **Do you have any questions about the chart?**

What evidence of positive goals and behavior do you see with your children?

How can you apply the concepts of this chart to the behavior of your own children, particularly the child who presents the most challenges for you?

7. Problem Situation

The Problem Situation gives parents an opportunity to put this session's ideas into practice. Ask participants to read the Problem Situation at the end of Chapter 1 in *The Parent's Handbook*. Then discuss the questions.

If time permits, you may want to have parents role-play this situation.

8. Summary

The summary is an important part of each session. It gives each parent an opportunity to identify and clarify what he or she is learning. It also gives the leader an opportunity to determine what the parents are learning and to get reactions to the way sessions are being conducted.

The summary may deal either with the session's instructional content or with the feelings of group members about the material.

Begin the summary by asking, **What did you learn from this meeting?** or **What do you think about the ideas presented in this session?**

9. Activity for the Week

For the coming week, ask parents to observe individual children and to analyze misbehavior in terms of the four goals discussed in this session. Ask them to notice *exactly:*

a. What the child did.

b. Their own feelings about the child's action.

c. The action they took.

d. The child's reaction to their response.

e. The apparent purpose of the misbehavior.

Also ask the parents to look for and encourage children's positive behavior. Tell the group that next week they will have an opportunity to discuss their experiences.

Remind parents that there are three aids in *The Parent's Handbook* that are designed to help them put the program into practice at home. As you point out its purpose, ask them to find each of the following items at the end of Chapter 1:

- *Charts 1A and 1B* are included in the handbook to serve as summaries of the major ideas covered in this session.
- *Points to Remember* is a list to remind them of the session's major points. Parents may want to cut it out and post it at home, perhaps on a bulletin board or the refrigerator.
- *My Plan for Improving Relationships* is a form on which parents can write down their concerns and assess their progress. Emphasize that this form is for private use, and is not something they will be asked to report on or discuss at a later session. Parents can also cut out this form.

10. Reading Assignment

Ask parents to read "Understanding More about Your Child and about Yourself as a Parent," Chapter 2 in *The Parent's Handbook,* before the next session. They may also want to read the Problem Situation and think about the questions accompanying it.

Tell them the reading will provide information on three concepts:

- How parents and children use their emotions
- How an individual's personality is formed
- Some mistaken ideas about what it means to be a "good" parent

Stress the value of doing the activity and the reading. Reiterate the need for study, plus observation and follow-up, if parents are to achieve the maximum benefit from the program.

Understanding How Children Use Emotions to Involve Parents *and* The "Good" Parent

Materials

- *The Parent's Handbook:* Chapter 2, "Understanding More about Your Child and about Yourself as a Parent"
- Videocassette 1 *or* Audiocassette 2, Side A: "Emotions Serve a Purpose"
- *Script Booklet*: Session 2 Tapescript
- Discussion Guidelines Poster
- Chart 2: Differences Between the "Good" Parent and the Responsible Parent

Objectives

The first part of the session focuses on ways children use negative emotions for one or more of the four goals—attention, power, revenge, and display of inadequacy. Parents will begin to learn how to avoid being trapped by their children's negative feelings.

The remainder of the session deals with fallacies of the concept of a "good" parent. Participants may be surprised that many commonly accepted attitudes considered desirable for being a "good" parent often influence children to be disrespectful, dependent, and irresponsible. Participants will learn to recognize some of the ways a parent can interfere with a child's development by attempting to do "the right thing."

Procedures

1. Discussion of the Activity for the Week

Discuss the Activity for the Week from Session 1: Parents were to observe their child or children and analyze any negative behavior in terms of the four goals of misbehavior. They were also to look for positive, goal-directed behavior.

Ask who would like to tell about the past week's experiences. Since this is the first opportunity to report on an activity assignment, it is very important to establish an expectation that all members will have done the activities. Encourage any positive efforts parents have made; it is important to recognize any evidence of progress. If anyone has had difficulty analyzing behavior in terms of the four goals, you may want to review the key concepts briefly.

2. Discussion of the Reading Assignment

The reading assignment for this session was "Understanding More about Your Child and about Yourself as a Parent," Chapter 2 in *The Parent's Handbook.* Use one of the following procedures to discuss the reading.

Alternative A. You can begin an open discussion by asking, **What did you learn from this reading?** and **How would you apply these ideas?** or, **Do you have any questions about the reading?** This should initiate a discussion that follows the group's interests. Discussion should focus on:

1. What the ideas and principles mean, and

2. Ways to apply these ideas and principles.

Alternative B. If you prefer a more organized format, use the following questions. These questions are supplied as guidelines; they are not intended to limit discussion. Alter the wording to suit your own style.

1. Do you ever use your emotions to influence other people? How?

2. How do children use emotions in negative ways?

3. What did you learn about sensitive children?

4. In general, how can we behave effectively when children are using their feelings in order to accomplish one of the goals of misbehavior?

5. What is meant by "lifestyle"?

   - Why are our beliefs about ourselves and others often faulty?

   - What are the four major factors which influence a person's lifestyle?

   - What is meant by family atmosphere? Family values? Sex roles? Family constellation? Methods of training?

6. What tend to be the characteristics of the first child? Second child? Middle child? Youngest child? Only child?

7. Can you see the influence of the family constellation on your own children? In what ways?

8. What do the authors mean by the "good" parent? How does a "good" parent behave?

9. Why do "good" parents behave as they do? What are the consequences for their children?

10. What is meant by the "responsible" parent? How do responsible parents behave? What are the consequences for their children?

Note: Chart 2, focusing on the differences between the "good" and the responsible parent, is discussed later in the session.

3. Presentation of Tape

The taped segment for this session is on Videocassette 1 *or* Audiocassette 2, Side A. Turn in your *Script Booklet* to the tapescript for Session 2 and follow the directions for conducting the taped presentation and discussion.

4. Discussion of the Tape

At the end of the tape, a number of people may be ready to ask questions. The preferred method of discussion is to follow topics raised by group members. However, if members are not ready to ask questions, you can begin the discussion with an open question: **What do you think about the ideas we heard and discussed here?**

If the group needs more direction, consider these topics:

a. The purposive nature of human emotions.

b. How children use feelings to achieve one or more of the four goals of misbehavior.

c. The concept of "water power."

d. Responding to temper tantrums.

e. How to encourage a child who feels like giving up.

f. The effect of pity on a child.

g. What is meant by the term "good" parent?

h. What motivates "good" parents?

i. Society's role in producing "good" parents.

j. The effect of the "good" parent on children.

k. The concept of mutual respect.

l. Protecting children by helping them learn to protect themselves.

5. Chart 2: Differences Between the "Good" Parent and the Responsible Parent

Take a few minutes to display and discuss Chart 2, using wording similar to the following:

The left side of this chart describes the "good" parent. The first column describes some typical beliefs held by "good" parents. The next column presents some typical parent behaviors related to each belief. The third column describes possible outcomes for the child that are related to each belief and behavior of the "good" parent.

Go over each example on the "Good" Parent side of the chart. Then ask: **Do you have any questions about the "Good" Parent side of the chart?**

Do you recognize yourself as holding any of these beliefs? Which ones?

Now let's look at the Responsible Parent side of the chart. The first column describes some beliefs of the responsible parent. The second column lists related behaviors, and the last column lists possible outcomes for the child. Notice that each belief, related parent behavior, and result for the child on the "Good" Parent side has a more appropriate counterpart on the Responsible Parent side.

Go over each example of the Responsible Parent side. Then ask: **Do you have any questions about the Responsible Parent side of the chart?**

Do you see how you might begin to change a "good" parent belief to a more positive responsible parent belief?

Ask parents to give examples of challenges they are experiencing with their own children that involve beliefs and behaviors characteristic of the "good" parent, and to suggest how they might change these. The group may brainstorm some suggestions.

6. Problem Situation

The Problem Situation gives parents an opportunity to put this session's ideas into practice. Ask participants to read the Problem Situation at the end of Chapter 2 in *The Parent's Handbook*. Then discuss the questions.

If time permits, you may want to have parents role-play this situation.

7. Summary

The summary is an important part of each session. It gives each parent an opportunity to identify and clarify what she or he is learning. It also gives the leader an opportunity to determine what the parents are learning and to get reactions to the way sessions are being conducted.

The summary may deal either with the session's instructional content or with the feelings of group members about the material.

Begin the summary by asking **What did you learn from this meeting?** or **What do you think about the ideas presented in this session?**

8. Activity for the Week

For the coming week, ask parents to analyze their children's emotional displays in terms of the four goals of misbehavior and to use what they have learned in this session to influence their children.

Also, ask them to watch for a situation in which they are about to be trapped into being a "good" parent and to take steps to avoid it. Tell the group that next week they will have an opportunity to discuss their experiences.

Remind parents that there are three aids in *The Parent's Handbook* that are designed to help them put the program into practice at home:

- *Chart 2* is included in the handbook to serve as a summary of the major ideas covered in this session.
- *Points to Remember* is a list to remind them of the session's major points. Parents may want to cut it out and post it at home, perhaps on a bulletin board or the refrigerator.
- *My Plan for Improving Relationships* is a form on which parents can write down their concerns and assess their progress. Emphasize that this form is for private use, and is not something they will be asked to report on or discuss at a later session. Parents can also cut out this form.

9. Reading Assignment

Ask parents to read "Encouragement: Building Your Child's Confidence and Feelings of Worth," Chapter 3 of *The Parent's Handbook,* before the next session. Tell them that it may provide some new information about the meaning of encouragement.

Session 3

Encouragement

Materials

- *The Parent's Handbook:* Chapter 3, "Encouragement: Building Your Child's Confidence and Feelings of Worth"
- Videocassette 1 *or* Audiocassette 2, Side B: "Encouragement"
- *Script Booklet:* Session 3 Tapescript
- Discussion Guidelines Poster
- Chart 3: Differences Between Praise and Encouragement
- Pencils and paper

Objectives

This session is concerned with helping parents understand the concept and the process of encouragement. It will point out the differences between praise and encouragement. It will also help parents differentiate between attitudes and behaviors that discourage, and attitudes and behaviors that encourage their children.

Procedures

1. Discussion of the Activity for the Week

Discuss the Activity for the Week from Session 2: Parents were to analyze their children's emotional displays in terms of the four goals of misbehavior and use what they learned in Session 2 to deal with emotional displays more effectively. They were also asked to watch for situations where they were tempted to play the role of the "good" parent and to take steps to avoid it.

Ask who would like to tell about his or her experiences. Encourage any positive efforts parents have made; it is important to recognize any evidence of progress. If anyone has had difficulty putting a concept into practice, you may want to review the concept briefly.

2. Discussion of the Reading Assignment

The reading assignment for this session was "Encouragement: Building Your Child's Confidence and Feelings of Worth," Chapter 3 in *The Parent's Handbook.* Use one of the following procedures to discuss the reading.

Alternative A. You can begin an open discussion by asking, **What did you learn from this reading?** and **How would you apply these ideas?** or, **Do you have any questions about the reading?** This should initiate a discussion that follows the group's interests. Discussion should focus on:

1. What the ideas and principles mean, and

2. Ways to apply these ideas and principles.

Alternative B. If you prefer a more organized format, use the following questions. These questions are supplied as guidelines; they are not intended to limit discussion.

1. What is meant by "encouragement"? How does encouragement affect a child's feeling about himself or herself?

2. How can negative expectations lead to poor performances?

3. What effects can the imposition of unreasonably high standards have on children?

4. How does reinforcing competition between brothers and sisters usually affect them?

5. What can be the results of overambition?

6. How do double standards affect the relationship between parents and children?

7. What is the meaning of "Accept your children as they are, not only as they could be"? Why is this important?

8. How does your attention to tattling give a discouraging message to the one who tattles as well as the one who is tattled on?

9. What is the difference between praise and encouragement? When can praise be encouraging or discouraging?

10. How are the examples of "The Special Language of Encouragement" different from words of praise?

11. Why is it important to recognize effort and improvement and not just accomplishment?

12. What are some ways you could encourage your child? (Ask for specific examples.)

13. Now let's look at the comparisons between our ideals and what we really do, on page 33 in your handbook. Which statements do you feel characterize your relations with your own children?

3. Chart 3: Differences Between Praise and Encouragement

Take a few minutes to display and discuss Chart 3, using wording similar to the following:

The left side of this chart describes praise. The first column tells the underlying characteristics of praise. The next column describes the message the child picks up from each characteristic of praise. The third column describes the probable outcomes for the child.

Go over each section on the Praise side of the chart. Then ask: **Do you have any questions about this side of the chart?**

What do you think about this explanation of praise?

Now let's look at the Encouragement side of the chart. The first column gives the underlying characteristics of encouragement. The next column lists the messages sent to the child, and the last column describes the probable outcomes for the child. Notice that each underlying characteristic, message, and outcome on the Praise side has a more appropriate counterpart on the Encouragement side.

Go over each section on the Encouragement side of the chart. Then ask: **Do you have any questions about the Encouragement side?**

How can you apply the information on this chart to the encouragement of your own children? (Ask parents to be specific.)

4. Presentation of Tape

The taped segment for this session is on Videocassette 1 *or* Audiocassette 2, Side B. Turn in your *Script Booklet* to the tapescript for Session 3 and follow the directions for conducting the taped presentation and discussion.

5. Discussion of the Tape

At the end of the tape, a number of people may be ready to ask questions. The preferred method of discussion is to follow topics raised by group members. However, if members are not ready to ask questions, you can begin the discussion with an open question: **What do you think about the ideas we heard and discussed here?**

If the group needs more direction, consider these topics:

a. The meaning of encouragement.

b. The differences between praise and encouragement.

c. Subtle ways to discourage children.

d. The difference between finding assets and finding faults.

6. Exercise

Ask parents to turn to the Exercise at the end of Chapter 3 in *The Parent's Handbook*. Ask them to construct encouraging responses for Situation 1. You may want to have members write their responses and then share them with the group. After everyone has finished, discuss the responses. Allow a few minutes for parents to react to the suggested responses. Then, as time and interest permit, have them construct and discuss encouraging responses for Situations 2, 3, 4, and 5 in turn.

Situation 1
Encouraging responses:
If you feel she can handle her arithmetic simply by increased effort:
- *"I know it's difficult, but you've been able to solve such problems before."*
- *"Keep trying. You'll make it!" Or, "You'll figure it out."*

If you feel the child really needs some help:
- *"Let's think this through together."*

As you're helping:
- *"That's right, you're getting it."*

Responses to avoid:
- *Demanding that the child "use her head"*
- *Giving in and doing the problem for her*

Situation 2
Encouraging responses focus on effort:
- *"I'm glad you're learning to dress yourself."*
- *"I'll bet you feel proud of yourself, getting dressed without any help!"*

Responses to avoid:
- *Insincere praise*
- *Showing the child the right way*

(If you feel the child needs lessons in dressing, at another time—a time which has been set aside for that purpose—you can make a game out of learning to dress that will be fun for both you and the child.)

Situation 3
Encouraging responses focus on the child's contribution and how helpful it was, rather than commenting on how well the job was performed:
- *"Thanks for your help. You made my job easier."*
- *"I appreciate your help, Johnny."*

Situation 4
Encouraging responses indicate confidence in the boy:
- *"It's a challenge, but I'm sure you can handle it."*

Or, the parent could make a suggestion in the form of a question:
- *"If you don't believe you'll do very well, what can you do to feel more comfortable about the recital?"*

Situation 5
Encouraging responses comment on something the girl did well:
- *"I liked the way you returned the serve in the second game."*
- *"Your backhand is improving."*

Responses to avoid:
- *Pointing out shortcomings*
- *Dwelling on the girl's mistakes*

Then hold a brief discussion of the following question:

How can you avoid giving praise when your child asks for it? Suppose your child brings you a perfect spelling paper expecting praise. What would you say? Allow time for responses.

Encouraging responses acknowledge how the child feels:
- *"It looks as if you're really proud of that paper."*
- *"It looks like you enjoyed doing that."*

Or focus on the effort:
- *"You really worked hard on that."*

7. Role-Play

Say: **Now we'll do another exercise to help you further understand the concept of encouragement. We will need two people to role-play the following scene: One volunteer will be a parent teaching a teenager (the second volunteer) to drive. This is the teenager's first lesson.**

Select two volunteers.

(Note: For the parent role, choose someone you feel will be a good actor. Take the person aside and instruct him or her to be very demanding, critical, and unsympathetic with the teenager.)

Arrange two chairs to simulate the front seat of a car. When the scene begins, there will probably be laughing and joking, as this is a new experience. Do not stop the scene until you think the players and the remainder of the group are recognizing the seriousness of what is happening. Then ask the group:

1. What did you observe happening?

2. If you were the teenager, how would you feel?

Next, ask the volunteer who played the teenager to describe how she or he felt.

After the discussion, ask for another volunteer to replay the role of parent. This time, the person is to encourage the teenager.

Allow each volunteer a couple of minutes. After each scene, ask the group what they observed and how they would feel if they were the teenager. Then ask the volunteer playing the teenager to describe what he or she was feeling as each parent attempted to be encouraging.

Finally, ask the group to discuss the value of this exercise in their relationships with their own children.

8. Problem Situation

The Problem Situation gives parents an opportunity to put this session's ideas into practice. Ask participants to read the Problem Situation at the end of Chapter 3 in *The Parent's Handbook*. Then discuss the questions.

If time permits, you may want to have parents role-play this situation.

9. Summary

The summary is an important part of each session. It gives each parent an opportunity to identify and clarify what he or she is learning. It also gives the leader an opportunity to determine what the parents are learning and to get reactions to the way sessions are being conducted.

The summary may deal either with the session's instructional content or with the feelings of group members about the material.

Begin the summary by asking, **What did you learn from this meeting?** or **What do you think about the ideas presented in this session?**

10. Activity for the Week

For the coming week, ask parents to find ways to encourage their children. Tell the group that next week they will have an opportunity to discuss their experiences.

Remind parents that there are three aids in *The Parent's Handbook* that are designed to help them put the program into practice at home:

- *Chart 3* is included in the handbook to serve as a summary of the major ideas covered in this session.
- *Points to Remember* is a list to remind them of the session's major points. Parents may want to cut it out and post it at home, perhaps on a bulletin board or the refrigerator.
- *My Plan for Improving Relationships* is a form on which parents can write down their concerns and assess their progress. Emphasize that this form is for private use, and is not something they will be asked to report on or discuss at a later session. Parents can also cut out this form.

11. Reading Assignment

Ask parents to read "Communication: How to Listen to Your Child," Chapter 4 in *The Parent's Handbook,* before the next session. Tell them it will describe the discouraging roles parents play when responding to children's feelings, and show how to respond so that lines of communication can be kept open.

Session 4

Communication: Listening

Materials

- *The Parent's Handbook:* Chapter 4, "Communication: How to Listen to Your Child"
- Videocassette 1 *or* Audiocassette 3, Side A: "Effective Listening"
- *Script Booklet*: Session 4 Tapescript
- Discussion Guidelines Poster
- Chart 4: Effective Listening
- Pencils and paper

Objectives

This lesson is designed to help parents improve their listening skills with their children. Participants will learn how to communicate to children that they understand the children's feelings.

Procedures

1. Discussion of the Activity for the Week

Discuss the Activity for the Week from Session 3: Parents were to find specific ways to encourage their children. Ask who would like to tell about his or her experiences. Encourage any positive efforts parents have made; it is important to recognize any evidence of progress. If anyone has had difficulty putting a concept into practice, you may want to review the concept briefly.

2. Discussion of the Reading Assignment

The reading assignment for this session was "Communication: How to Listen to Your Child," Chapter 4 in *The Parent's Handbook.* Use one of the following procedures to discuss the reading.

Alternative A. You can begin an open discussion by asking, **What did you learn from this reading?** and **How would you apply these ideas?** or, **Do you have any questions about the reading?** This should initiate a discussion that follows the group's interests. Discussion should focus on:

1. What the ideas and principles mean, and

2. Ways to apply these ideas and principles.

Alternative B. If you prefer a more organized format, use the following questions. These questions are supplied as guidelines; they are not intended to limit discussion.

1. What is suggested by the recommendation to treat our children as friends?

2. The authors mention seven traditional roles adults play when responding to children's feelings. Do you notice yourself playing any of these roles? Which ones?

3. What is involved in being a good listener?

4. What is reflective listening? In what sorts of situations would it be useful with your children?

5. What is meant by a "closed response"? Can you think of some examples of closed responses other than those given by the authors?

6. What is meant by an "open response"? Can you think of examples of open responses other than those given by the authors?

7. What is the difference between closed and open responses in terms of their effect on the child?

8. What do the authors mean by "listening" to behavior?

9. How can you influence children to discuss their feelings when their nonverbal behavior indicates that they are upset?

10. How is reflective listening different from parroting?

11. How is a reflective listening response constructed?

12. What are some of the cautions the authors mentioned about using reflective listening?

3. Chart 4: Effective Listening

Take a few minutes to display and discuss Chart 4, using wording similar to the following:

At the top of this chart there are definitions of "closed" and "open" responses. The left-hand column gives statements that a child might say to a parent. The next column illustrates closed responses, and the last column illustrates alternative, open responses.

Go over each example on the chart. Then ask: **Do you have any questions about the chart so far?**

Under the examples of children's remarks and closed and open responses, the chart contains additional child statements without parental responses.

Ask: **What would be an example of a closed response to a child who says, "I don't like vegetables, and I'm not going to eat them"? What would be an open response?**

Repeat this procedure for each of the other statements. You may wish to refer parents to the Feeling Word List in *The Parent's Handbook* and to the section "How to Construct a Reflective Listening Response."

4. Presentation of Tape

The taped segment for this session is on Videocassette 1 *or* Audiocassette 3, Side A. Turn in your *Script Booklet* to the tapescript for Session 4 and follow the directions for conducting the taped presentation and discussion.

5. Discussion of the Tape

At the end of the tape, a number of people may be ready to ask questions. The preferred method of discussion is to follow topics raised by group members. However, if members are not ready to ask questions, you can begin the discussion with an open question: **What do you think about the ideas we heard and discussed here?**

If the group needs more direction, consider these topics:

a. How listening improves communication.

b. Why we don't listen well.

c. Reflective listening.

d. The difference between open and closed responses.

6. Role-Play

Tell the group that they are going to be sending "feeling messages" about their experiences as parents. (You may want to model the process by sending the first message.)

Ask a member (Parent A) to describe an experience to the person (Parent B) on his or her left. The topic can be anything that Parent A has some feeling about. Parent B will listen reflectively and give an open response to the statement of Parent A.

Ask the group to classify Parent B's response as open or closed and to give the reasons for their ratings.

Then proceed around the circle, with Parent B sending a feeling message to Parent C, and so on. The group should identify each response as open or closed.

Go around the circle as many times as time permits.

After group members have practiced reflective listening with each other, ask:

- **How did it feel to receive a *closed* response?**
- **How did it feel to receive an *open* response?**
- **How did it feel to *give* an open response?**
- **Did you learn anything from this experience? What?**

7. Problem Situation

The Problem Situation gives parents an opportunity to put this session's ideas into practice. Ask participants to read the Problem Situation at the end of Chapter 4 in *The Parent's Handbook*. Then discuss the questions.

If time permits, you may want to have parents role-play this situation.

8. Summary

The summary is an important part of each session. It gives each parent an opportunity to identify and clarify what she or he is learning. It also gives the leader an opportunity to determine what the parents are learning and to get reactions to the way sessions are being conducted.

The summary may deal either with the session's instructional content or with the feelings of group members about the material.

Begin the summary by asking, **What did you learn from this meeting?** or **What do you think about the ideas presented in this session?**

9. Activity for the Week

For the coming week, ask parents to practice reflective listening with their children. Tell the group that next week they will have a chance to discuss their experiences.

Remind parents that there are three aids in *The Parent's Handbook* that are designed to help them put the program into practice at home:

- *Chart 4* is included in the handbook to serve as a summary of the major ideas covered in this session.
- *Points to Remember* is a list to remind them of the session's major points. Parents may want to cut it out and post it at home, perhaps on a bulletin board or the refrigerator.
- *My Plan for Improving Relationships* is a form on which parents can write down their concerns and assess their progress. Emphasize that this form is for private use, and is not something they will be asked to report on or discuss at a later session. Parents can also cut out this form.

10. Reading Assignment

Ask parents to read "Communication: Exploring Alternatives and Expressing Your Ideas and Feelings to Children," Chapter 5 of *The Parent's Handbook,* before the next session. Tell them it will provide ideas about helping their children to explore alternatives and getting their children to listen to them.

Communication: Exploring Alternatives and Expressing Your Ideas and Feelings to Children

Materials

- *The Parent's Handbook:* Chapter 5, "Communication: Exploring Alternatives and Expressing Your Ideas and Feelings to Children"
- Videocassette 2 *or* Audiocassette 3, Side B: "Problem Ownership and I-Messages"
- *Script Booklet*: Session 5 Tapescript
- Discussion Guidelines Poster
- Chart 5: Decisions for Effective Communication
- Pencils and paper

Objectives

This lesson will help parents understand three concepts: exploring alternatives, problem ownership, and how to communicate their feelings to children in a nonthreatening way.

Procedures

1. Discussion of the Activity for the Week

Discuss the Activity for the Week from Session 4: Parents were to practice reflective listening with their children. Ask who would like to tell about his or her experiences with reflective listening. Encourage any positive efforts parents have made; it is important to recognize any evidence of progress. If anyone has had difficulty putting a concept into practice, you may want to review the concept briefly.

2. Discussion of the Reading Assignment

The reading assignment for this session was "Communication: Exploring Alternatives and Expressing Your Ideas and Feelings to Children," Chapter 5 in *The Parent's Handbook.* Use one of the following procedures to discuss the reading.

Alternative A. You can begin an open discussion by asking, **What did you learn from this reading?** and **How would you apply these ideas?** or, **Do you have any questions about the reading?** This should initiate a discussion that follows the group's interests. Discussion should focus on:

1. What the ideas and principles mean, and

2. Ways to apply these ideas and principles.

Alternative B. If you prefer a more organized format, use the following questions. These questions are supplied as guidelines; they are not intended to limit discussion.

1. What is meant by "exploring alternatives"?

2. How does exploring alternatives differ from giving advice? Why is giving advice often ineffective?

3. What are the steps in exploring alternatives?

4. What can you do when your child is not able to generate ideas due to lack of experience?

5. When should you enter into exploring alternatives with your child?

6. What do the authors mean by "problem ownership"? Why is it important to recognize who owns the problem?

7. Why don't children listen to their parents?

8. What is an "I-message"? How is an I-message different from a "you-message"?

9. How is an I-message constructed? Why is it important to communicate to the child that the consequence of his or her behavior is what is disturbing you, rather than the behavior itself?

10. Why do parents use sarcasm and ridicule? What are the effects of these disciplinary methods on the child and on the parent?

11. How do your beliefs about your children affect your communication with them? How can you communicate your faith in your children?

3. Chart 5: Decisions for Effective Communication

Take a few minutes to display and discuss Chart 5, using wording similar to the following:

The first column on the left gives situations involving parent or child problems. The next column tells who owns the problem—whether it's the parent's problem or the child's problem. The third and fourth columns illustrate reflective listening responses for the child-owned problems and I-messages for the parent-owned problems.

Go over each example on the chart. Then ask: **Do you have any questions about this chart?**

4. Presentation of Tape

The taped segment for this session is on Videocassette 2 *or* Audiocassette 3, Side B. Turn in your *Script Booklet* to the tapescript for Session 5 and follow the directions for conducting the taped presentation and discussion.

5. Discussion of the Tape

At the end of the tape, a number of people may be ready to ask questions. The preferred method of discussion is to follow topics raised by group members.

However, if members are not ready to ask questions, you can begin the discussion with an open question: **What do you think about the ideas we heard and discussed here?**

If the group needs more direction, consider these topics:

a. Using reflective listening to understand and clarify the child's feelings.

b. Exploring alternatives through brainstorming.

c. Assisting the child in choosing a solution.

d. Discussing the probable results of the child's decision.

e. Obtaining a commitment.

f. Planning a time for evaluation.

g. The meaning of "problem ownership."

h. Guidelines for determining problem ownership.

i. "Parent deafness."

j. You-messages—what they are and why they don't work.

k. I-messages—what they are and how to phrase them.

l. Talking with your children as you would to your friends.

6. Role-Play

Ask for two volunteers to demonstrate exploring alternatives. One volunteer will present a problem—something that's bothering him or her about a child. The other volunteer will help the first one explore alternatives, keeping the six steps in mind while helping the first person develop a solution. The group may provide assistance, if needed. If necessary, refer parents to the six steps in *The Parent's Handbook*. Ask the group to evaluate the process when the dialogue is concluded.

7. Exercises

Ask the group to turn to Exercises 1 and 2 at the end of Chapter 5 in *The Parent's Handbook*. Give them the following instructions for Exercise 1.

Say: **As you do this exercise, disregard the fact that you might be assuming responsibility for your child's problems. Mark a "C" if your child is the real owner of the problem, and a "P" if the problem belongs to you.**

Allow parents a few minutes to complete the exercise. After they have finished, allow time for comparing responses.

Problems involving fights with brothers and sisters, misbehavior at school, homework, bedtime, morning routine, peers—numbers 2, 4, 5, 6, 7, and 10—are really owned by the children involved. It is only if a problem genuinely interferes with the parent's rights or threatens the safety of the child that it would be classified as owned by the parent.

The remainder of the problems—misbehavior in public, leaving belongings around the house, messing up the kitchen, misbehavior at the dinner table (numbers 1, 3, 8, and 9)—are examples of problems owned by the parent, because clearly they interfere with the parent's rights.

Possible ways to deal with parent-owned problems:
- *Ignore the act*
- *Employ natural or logical consequences (a technique discussed in later sessions)*
- *Engage in problem-solving discussions with the child*
- *Let the child know how you feel*

Next, ask the group to turn to Exercise 2 and review the three parts of an I-message. Then ask participants to design an I-message for each of the five practice situations listed in the exercise. You may want to point out that each situation is a parent-owned problem. Suggest to them that they start by thinking of one word to express how they feel about the situation; they can refer to the Feeling Word List in Chapter Four of the handbook if they wish. You may want to have members write their I-messages and read them to the group.

Possible responses:
Situation 1: "When you back out of the driveway that fast, I get very concerned because you might get hurt or hurt someone else."

Situation 2: "When I expect help and don't get it, I really feel rushed, because I get behind."

Situation 3: "When I see mud on the car I just washed, I really feel discouraged because I have to clean it again."

Situation 4: "When the dog doesn't get fed, I feel sorry for him, because I know how it feels to be hungry."

Situation 5: "When the brush isn't put in turpentine right after it's used, I get worried because the paint will harden and I'll have to buy a new brush."

Responses to avoid:
- *Angry I-messages that "blast" the child—these have the effect of a you-message*

8. Problem Situation

The Problem Situation gives parents an opportunity to put this session's ideas into practice. Ask participants to read the Problem Situation at the end of Chapter 5 in *The Parent's Handbook*. Then discuss the questions.

If time permits, you may want to have parents role-play this situation.

9. Summary

The summary is an important part of each session. It gives each parent an opportunity to identify and clarify what he or she is learning. It also gives the leader an opportunity to determine what the parents are learning and to get reactions to the way sessions are being conducted.

The summary may deal either with the session's instructional content or with the feelings of group members about the material.

Begin the summary by asking, **What did you learn from this meeting?** or **What do you think about the ideas presented in this session?**

10. Activity for the Week

For the coming week, ask parents to help their children explore alternatives—if they feel the children are ready—and to practice using I-messages. Tell the group that next week they will have a chance to discuss their experiences.

Remind parents that there are three aids in *The Parent's Handbook* that are designed to help them put the program into practice at home:

- *Chart 5* is included in the handbook to serve as a summary of the major ideas covered in this session.
- *Points to Remember* is a list to remind them of the session's major points. Parents may want to cut it out and post it at home, perhaps on a bulletin board or the refrigerator.
- *My Plan for Improving Relationships* is a form on which parents can write down their concerns and assess their progress. Emphasize that this form is for private use, and is not something they will be asked to report on or discuss at a later session. Parents can also cut out this form.

11. Reading Assignment

Ask parents to read "Natural and Logical Consequences: A Method of Discipline That Develops Responsibility," Chapter 6 of *The Parent's Handbook,* before the next session. Tell them that this reading will provide them with new ideas about how to win their children's cooperation.

Session 6

Developing Responsibility

Materials

- *The Parent's Handbook:* Chapter 6, "Natural and Logical Consequences: A Method of Discipline That Develops Responsibility"
- Videocassette 2 *or* Audiocassette 4, Side A: "Disciplining with Consequences"
- *Script Booklet*: Session 6 Tapescript
- Discussion Guidelines Poster
- Chart 6: The Major Differences Between Punishment and Logical Consequences
- Pencils and paper

Objectives

This lesson is designed to help parents recognize the differences between autocratic, permissive, and democratic methods of gaining cooperation from their children. Parents will become familiar with the concepts of natural and logical consequences—democratic procedures that replace reward and punishment as a way of discipline. Participants will also learn procedures for using natural and logical consequences and learn how to distinguish between logical consequences and punishment.

Procedures

1. Discussion of the Activity for the Week

Discuss the Activity for the Week from Session 5: Parents were to help their children explore alternatives and to practice sending I-messages to their children. Ask who would like to tell about his or her experience. Encourage any positive efforts parents have made; it is important to recognize any evidence of progress. If anyone has had difficulty putting a concept into practice, you may want to review the concept briefly.

2. Discussion of the Reading Assignment

The reading assignment for this session was "Natural and Logical Consequences: A Method of Discipline That Develops Responsibility," Chapter 6 of *The Parent's Handbook*. Use one of the following procedures to discuss the reading.

Alternative A. You can begin an open discussion by asking, **What did you learn from this reading?** and **How would you apply these ideas?** or, **Do you have any questions about the reading?** This should initiate a discussion that follows the group's interests. Discussion should focus on:

1. What the ideas and principles mean, and

2. Ways to apply these ideas and principles.

Alternative B. If you prefer a more organized format, use the following questions. These questions are supplied as guidelines; they are not intended to limit discussion.

1. Why do the authors suggest doing away with reward and punishment as a way to relate to children?

2. What alternatives to reward and punishment do the authors suggest?

3. Why are natural and logical consequences more effective than reward and punishment?

4. What is the difference between a natural consequence and a logical consequence?

5. The authors give the following examples of natural consequences:

   • The child who refuses to eat goes hungry.

   • The child who does not wear mittens has cold hands.

   Can you think of a challenge with your own children for which natural consequences would apply? (Ask parents to give examples other than those in the handbook.)

6. When should logical consequences be used instead of natural consequences?

7. How do logical consequences differ from punishment?

8. How can consequences be turned into punishment?

9. Why is it important to understand the child's goal and feelings before applying consequences?

10. What is meant by being *both* firm and kind?

11. Why is consistency important?

12. What is meant by "separating the deed from the doer"? Why is this principle important when using consequences?

13. Why is the principle "talk less, act more" important to remember?

14. What is meant by refusing either to fight or to give in?

15. Why is timing important in applying consequences?

16. Why is it important to let all the children involved in a problem share the responsibility?

17. What are the steps involved in applying consequences?

18. Can you think of a challenge with your child where logical consequences would apply?

3. Chart 6: The Major Differences Between Punishment and Logical Consequences

Take a few minutes to display and discuss Chart 6, using wording similar to the following:

The left side of this chart describes punishment. The first column tells the characteristics of punishment. The next column presents the underlying message to the child stemming from each characteristic. The third column describes the possible outcomes for the child.

Go over each section on the Punishment side of the chart. Then ask: **Do you have any questions about this side of the chart? What do you think about these ideas?**

Now let's look at the Logical Consequences side of the chart. The first column gives the characteristics of logical consequences. The next column describes the underlying message to the child, and the last column tells the probable outcome for the child. Notice that each characteristic, underlying message, and probable outcome for the child on the Punishment side has a positive counterpart on the Logical Consequences side.

Go over each section on the Logical Consequences side of the chart. Then ask: **Do you have any questions about the Logical Consequences side? How does this chart help you differentiate between punishment and logical consequences?**

Ask parents to design a consequence for one of their own child-training challenges and to describe how the consequence would differ from punishment.

4. Presentation of Tape

The taped segment for this session is on Videocassette 2 *or* Audiocassette 4, Side A. Turn in your *Script Booklet* to the tapescript for Session 6 and follow the directions for conducting the taped presentation and discussion.

5. Discussion of the Tape

At the end of the tape, a number of people may be ready to ask questions. The preferred method of discussion is to follow topics raised by group members. However, if members are not ready to ask questions, you can begin the discussion with an open question: **What do you think about the ideas we heard and discussed here?**

If the group needs more direction, consider these topics:

a. Differences between the autocratic, the permissive, and the democratic parent.

b. The difference between natural and logical consequences.

c. The major differences between punishment and logical consequences.

6. Exercise

Tell the group to read the directions for the Exercise at the end of Chapter 6 in *The Parent's Handbook* and to design natural or logical consequences for Practice Situation 1. You may want to have them write their consequences and read them to the group. Hold a brief discussion of the suggested consequences. Then, as time permits, have participants move on to design consequences for Practice Situations 2, 3, and 4 in turn.

Situation 1

There are several options Mr. and Mrs. Thompson might use for solving this problem:

- *Establish a lost-and-found box and put any items found lying around into the box. Parents who use this procedure usually find that the children remember to pick up their possessions when they have become tired of rummaging through the box.*
- *Tell the children that they, the parents, will pick up the articles and return them when the children's behavior indicates they are ready to assume responsibility for their possessions.*
- *Establish a time for pickup or cleanup when everyone pitches in; allow children to choose an area to work in. (Not recommended if the relationship between parents and children is not good.)*

Avoid reminders, threats, and hidden messages.

Situation 2

Possible solutions:

- *Parents negotiate a bedtime they and child can agree on.*
- *Parents tell the child, "All right, when it's that time, we will assume you're in bed."*
- *Parents let child be responsible for keeping track of the time. (Young children who cannot tell time can keep track of it from TV programs or with the "big-hand/little-hand" method.)*
- *When the agreed-upon time arrives, parents assume child is in bed and ignore any bids for attention or service. They should also ignore any attempts to provoke them. When ignored or left alone, most children soon discover that it isn't much fun to stay up late. Consequently, they become more responsible about bedtime.*

If a child tries to show power by refusing to observe a bedtime:

- *Allow the child to stay up as late as she or he pleases.*
- *Require the child to get up at the regular time and to carry out the activities of a regular day. Then lack of sleep becomes a natural consequence of not going to bed at a reasonable hour.*

If a child stays up and falls asleep on the couch or floor:

- *Leave the child there. If necessary, cover child with a blanket, but let child be responsible for getting to bed.*

Responses to avoid:

- *Giving negative attention*
- *Ordering the child to bed*

Situation 3

Possible solutions:

- *Remove child's plate and say, "When you're ready to use table manners, you may continue to eat." Remain friendly and continue to include Barbara in the dinner conversation.*
- *If Barbara still does not observe table manners when her plate is returned, remove the plate and say, "I see you're still not ready. You may try again at breakfast."*

- *If Barbara is unwilling to observe table manners at breakfast, remove the plate and say, "You may try again at lunch." Give no further explanation.*
- *If it happens again at lunch, remove Barbara's plate with no explanation—no talking—at all.*

General guidelines for dealing with the problem:
- *Remain calm, firm, and kind.*
- *Minimize talking, and simply act, without fuss.*
- *Maintain a positive attitude.*
- *Make sure that snacks are not available; don't allow raiding the refrigerator. Otherwise, missing a meal will have not have natural consequence of hunger.*
- *Be consistent.*

Responses to avoid:
- *Reminding the child to observe manners at the dinner table*

Situation 4
Possible solutions:
- *Decide that the boys own the problem; allow them to work out their differences and to learn from the natural consequences of fighting.*
- *Refuse to get involved; if necessary, go into your bedroom or bathroom and lock the door. You may want to place a radio or TV in the room ahead of time to help drown out the noise. Or, you may prefer to take a walk or drive around the block.*

When parents avoid involvement:
- *The fighting may intensify.*
- *The fights may follow them to another part of the house.*
- *One child may pretend that he is hurt in order to get his parents to come to the rescue and blame the other child.*
- *The children may tattle on one another. The parents can help the tattler be responsible for his own part in the fight by replying, "The fight is between you and your brother. I'm sure you can handle it."*

Responses to avoid:
- *Interfering in the boys' fights*
- *Trying to find out who has started a fight*
- *Trying to identify and punish the so-called "guilty" child*
- *Punishing both offenders*
- *Fighting with the children about fighting*

Hold a brief discussion of the following questions about adult involvement in children's fights:

1. What about boys hitting girls?
Many parents believe that boys should not hit girls. Under this double standard, girls can "get away with murder" while boys pay for the crime. When parents allow brothers and sisters to settle their own conflicts through natural consequences, girls learn not to provoke their brothers.

2. Should younger children be expected to settle their conflicts with older siblings unassisted?
Unless there is a considerable age difference between older and younger children, it's more appropriate to allow older and younger children a chance to work out their own relationships.

When parents fear serious harm to younger children, it's best to remove them from the scene. Distracting them—that is, getting them interested in other things—is usually effective. Because young children do provoke their older brothers and sisters, the older ones shouldn't be blamed for becoming irritated. Removal of the "thorn in their side" without comment is usually sufficient.

3. What should one do if children are using dangerous objects in a fight?
Most children will not physically harm one another in a fight. Occasionally a child may become furious and pick up a dangerous object, such as a stick, a stone, or an ashtray, which could do harm. If this occurs, remove the object and inform the children that if they wish to fight, they can use their hands.

4. What should one do about children who physically fight in areas where they may hurt themselves or damage property?
Although it's usually best for parents to remove themselves from the battlefield of a fight between children, exceptions are:
* *When children are fighting in dangerous areas*
* *When damage could result to family property*
* *When children are fighting in areas of the house that a parent needs to occupy*

*At such times, logical consequences are in order: You may want to give them the choice of an alternate battlefield: "Either stop fighting or go outside and fight." If the children do not stop fighting after you have said this **only once,** calmly usher them out the door, saying, "I see you have decided to fight outside. When you're finished, you may come back in."*

5. What if children decide to start a fight while you are watching TV?
Use logical consequences as just described in question 4.

7. Problem Situation

The Problem Situation gives parents an opportunity to put this session's ideas into practice. Ask participants to read the Problem Situation at the end of Chapter 6 in *The Parent's Handbook*. Then discuss the questions.

If time permits, you may want to have parents role-play this situation.

8. Summary

The summary is an important part of each session. It gives each parent an opportunity to identify and clarify what she or he is learning. It also gives the leader an opportunity to determine what the parents are learning and to get reactions to the way sessions are being conducted.

The summary may deal either with the session's instructional content or with the feelings of group members about the material.

Begin the summary by asking, **What did you learn from this meeting?** or **What do you think about the ideas presented in this session?**

9. Activity for the Week

For the coming week, ask parents to practice applying natural or logical consequences to one of their child-training problems. They should choose a situation in which they believe they can be successful. Tell the group that next week they will have a chance to discuss their experiences.

Remind parents that there are three aids in *The Parent's Handbook* that are designed to help them put the program into practice at home:

- *Chart 6* is included in the handbook to serve as a summary of the major ideas covered in this session.
- *Points to Remember* is a list to remind them of the session's major points. Parents may want to cut it out and post it at home, perhaps on a bulletin board or the refrigerator.
- *My Plan for Improving Relationships* is a form on which parents can write down their concerns and assess their progress. Emphasize that this form is for private use, and is not something they will be asked to report on or discuss at a later session. Parents can also cut out this form.

10. Reading Assignment

Ask parents to read "Applying Natural and Logical Consequences to Other Concerns," Chapter 7 in *The Parent's Handbook,* before the next session. Tell them that it will provide additional information for handling specific challenges.

Session 7

Decision Making for Parents

Materials

- *The Parent's Handbook:* Chapter 7, "Applying Natural and Logical Consequences to Other Concerns"
- Videocassette 2 *or* Audiocassette 4, Side B: "Creating Logical Consequences"
- *Script Booklet*: Session 7 Tapescript
- Discussion Guidelines Poster
- Chart 7: Selecting the Appropriate Approach
- Pencils and paper

Objectives

This session is concerned with two aspects of child training. First, parents will learn how to stop reacting to provocations and to act deliberately instead. Second, they will learn how to choose among the approaches to effective child-rearing (reflective listening and exploring alternatives; I-messages; and natural and logical consequences).

Procedures

1. Discussion of the Activity for the Week

Discuss the Activity for the Week from Session 6: Parents were to apply the concept of natural or logical consequences to one of their child-training problems. Ask who would like to tell about his or her experiences. Encourage any positive efforts parents have made; it is important to recognize any evidence of progress. If anyone has had difficulty putting a concept into practice, you may want to review the concept briefly.

2. Discussion of the Reading Assignment

The reading assignment for this session was "Applying Natural and Logical Consequences to Other Concerns," Chapter 7 of *The Parent's Handbook.* Use one of the following procedures to discuss the reading. (Note: While discussing this reading assignment, be sure to review the concepts from Session 6. They are essential for understanding Session 7.)

Alternative A. You can begin an open discussion by asking, **What did you learn from this reading?** and **How would you apply these ideas?** or, **Do you have any questions about the reading?** This should initiate a discussion that follows the group's interests. Discussion should focus on:

1. What the ideas and principles mean, and

2. Ways to apply these ideas and principles.

Alternative B. If you prefer a more organized format, use the following questions. These questions are supplied as guidelines; they are not intended to limit discussion.

1. What are logical consequences? How are logical consequences different from punishment?

2. The authors present natural and logical consequences for typical challenges presented by children. As an example, let's talk about the child who frequently seems to forget things:

   - How do we usually react?

   - What would be an appropriate logical consequence, and why would it be more effective than the typical reactions are?

As time permits, discuss two or three more challenges presented in the reading.

Note: Because Chart 7 summarizes material, it is discussed later in the session.

3. Presentation of Tape

The taped segment for this session is on Videocassette 2 *or* Audiocassette 4, Side B. Turn in your *Script Booklet* to the tapescript for Session 7 and follow the directions for conducting the taped presentation and discussion.

4. Discussion of the Tape

At the end of the tape, a number of people may be ready to ask questions. The preferred method of discussion is to follow topics raised by group members. However, if members are not ready to ask questions, you can begin the discussion with an open question, **What do you think about the ideas we heard and discussed here?**

If your group needs more direction, consider these topics:

a. How doing what children expect reinforces their goals.

b. What is meant by the principle of "Acting—Not Reacting."

c. How parents can put the principle of "Acting—Not Reacting" into practice.

d. A parent's experience with the effectiveness of each approach helps determine the approach selected.

e. How problem ownership determines the approach to be used.

f. The limitations of reflective listening, exploring alternatives, and I-messages.

g. Situations that may require all three approaches.

h. Situations in which it is appropriate to ignore children's misbehavior.

5. Exercises

Have parents turn to Exercises 1 and 2 at the end of Chapter 7 in *The Parent's Handbook*. Ask them to decide on responses for Situation 1 in Exercise 1. You may want to have them write their responses and then share the responses with the group. When they have finished, hold a brief discussion of their responses. Then, as time permits, ask them to decide on and discuss responses for Situations 2, 3, and 4 in turn.

Situation 1
How to take action instead of reacting:
- *Let the child experience the logical consequences of spilling. You could say matter-of-factly, "You had an accident. Let's get a rag to clean it up." In this way the child would receive no "fringe benefits" of attention for negative behavior. He would merely experience the consequences.*

Situation 2
How to take action instead of reacting:
- *Firmly but kindly say no and let the child decide how to respond. If the child throws a tantrum, keep walking and busy yourself by looking at other items in the store. If you remain firm and calm, the child will sense that the behavior is not rewarding, and will give it up.*
- *Decline to take the child to the store the next time, and explain that the reason is that the child has not yet learned how to act in public. (If she is too young to be left by herself, arrange for someone to watch her.) Assure her that she will have a chance to go again when the next trip is planned.*
- *Respect children's wishes by giving them—when possible—the choice of going shopping or staying at home. That will increase the probability of cooperation when they must accompany you to the store.*

Situation 3
How to take action instead of reacting:
- *Tell the child that when you are finished talking, you will be glad to talk with him, and then ignore further interruptions.*
- *If the interruptions persist, move to another room to finish your conversation or, depending upon the child's age and the situation, offer him the choice of being quiet or leaving. "You may stay with us and wait until we are finished talking, or leave the room." Say no more.*
- *If the child refuses to leave, give the child a second choice: "Either go on your own, or I will take you out of the room."*
- *If necessary, simply take the child by the hand and lead him out. Remain friendly as well as firm.*

Situation 4
How to take action instead of reacting:
- *Use logical consequences by removing the bicycle and informing the child that she does not appear to be ready to be responsible for the bike, and will not be allowed to use the bike again until the next day.*
- *If the child leaves her bike on the driveway again, calmly remove the bike and state that it may not be used for two days.*

Next, have parents move on to Exercise 2. Ask them to decide on solutions for Practice Situation 1 in Exercise 2. You may want to have them write their solutions and then share the solutions with the group. When they have finished, hold a brief discussion of their solutions. Then, as time permits, have them decide on and discuss solutions for Practice Situations 2, 3, and 4 in turn.

Situation 1
- *You, the parent, own the problem.*
- *You could use either Approach 2 (I-messages) or Approach 3 (natural and logical consequences), or a combination of both.*
- *You might tell the children, "With all the noise, I can't concentrate on my book." Or you could use a logical consequence by giving the child a choice: "I can't read my book with all that noise. You may quiet down or go outside and play." If you decided to use an I-message but your communication was unsuccessful, you could proceed with a logical consequence. Present the alternatives in a friendly manner, and respect the children's choice. If they continue to be noisy, matter-of-factly follow through with, "I see you've decided to play outside. You may come back in, if you want to, after I have finished my reading."*

Situation 2
- *You, the parent, own the problem.*
- *You could use either an I-message or a logical consequence.*
- *You could say that you feel it does not make sense to pay for lessons unless they are used. Your I-message might be: "When you don't practice your guitar, I get concerned because I feel the money for lessons is wasted." Or, you could use a logical consequence and say: "I'm willing to pay for the lessons only if you are willing to practice. If you stop practicing, I'll assume that you've decided to stop taking lessons." This leaves the door open for her to resume lessons if she later becomes genuinely interested. Another alternative might be for you to discuss the idea of logical consequences with the guitar teacher. The teacher could inform your daughter that lessons would continue only if she practiced her guitar.*

Situation 3
- *The boy who has been hit must be allowed to own the problem if he is to develop problem-solving and social skills.*
- *You can assist him to cope with this difficult situation by utilizing Approach 1, reflective listening and exploring alternatives.*
- *Try reflecting his feelings: "You're feeling very bad and hurt," or, "You're really angry with Billy." After he responds to your reflective listening, help him explore alternatives with, "What do you think you can do next time?" or, "How do you think you can avoid being hit again?" If a child brings up the same or similar difficulties to you several times, the child has probably learned to use problems to gain your attention or sympathy. For this child it's best to discontinue reflective listening and exploring alternatives, and tell the child that she or he can handle the situation alone. You could say, "It looks as if this is a problem you can take care of by yourself. I'm sure you will find a way to handle it."*

Situation 4

- *You, the parent, own the problem.*
- *To resolve it, some of you may prefer I-messages, but most of you—because of the seriousness of the problem—are likely to prefer consequences.*
- *You could tell the child, "I came home early today and found the door unlocked. It doesn't look as if you're ready yet to be responsible for locking up the house. I'll have to take your key. For the next couple of days, you'll need to go to the child care center before and after school. In a couple of days you may use the key again so we can see if you are ready to be responsible."*

A word of caution about I-messages: If they're overused, children may become tired of hearing about the parent's feelings and stop listening. I-messages may also provide a way for children to obtain attention or trap the parent in a power struggle. If I-messages don't work, it may be a good idea to concentrate on consequences. This is especially true for problems that belong to the child only and do not involve the parent. Remember that ignoring behavior is one form of logical consequence because it prevents the child from receiving a payoff for misbehavior.

Deciding which approach to use takes practice. It also requires parents to know what works and what doesn't work with their children. With experience, parents will come to know which approaches are most effective for them.

6. Chart 7: Selecting the Appropriate Approach

Take a few minutes to display and discuss Chart 7, using wording similar to the following:

This chart pulls together the approaches we have learned thus far in the program. The first column on the left side gives examples of problems in parent-child relations. The next column tells who owns each problem. The last column gives examples of appropriate approaches, depending on who owns the problem—parent or child. Do you have any questions about the chart?

The chart also lists some problems without responses.

Ask: **In the first situation—the child who does not lock up his or her bicycle—who owns the problem? What would be an appropriate approach?**

Continue this procedure in discussing the other situations.

7. Problem Situation

The Problem Situation gives parents an opportunity to put this session's ideas into practice. Ask participants to read the Problem Situation at the end of Chapter 7 in *The Parent's Handbook*. Then discuss the questions.

If time permits, you may want to have parents role-play this situation.

8. Summary

The summary is an important part of each session. It gives each parent an opportunity to identify and clarify what he or she is learning. It also gives the leader an opportunity to determine what the parents are learning and to get reactions to the way sessions are being conducted.

The summary may deal either with the session's instructional content or with the feelings of group members about the material.

Begin the summary by asking, **What did you learn from this meeting?** or **What do you think about the ideas presented in this session?**

9. Activity for the Week

For the coming week, ask parents to choose a child-training challenge in which they have reinforced a child's misbehavior by doing what the child expects. The principle of "Acting—Not Reacting" should be used in planning an effective response. Tell the group that next week they will have a chance to discuss their experiences.

Remind parents that there are three aids in *The Parent's Handbook* that are designed to help them put the program into practice at home:

- *Chart 7* is included in the handbook to serve as a summary of the major ideas covered in this session.
- *Points to Remember* is a list to remind them of the session's major points. Parents may want to cut it out and post it at home, perhaps on a bulletin board or the refrigerator.
- *My Plan for Improving Relationships* is a form on which parents can write down their concerns and assess their progress. Emphasize that this form is for private use, and is not something they will be asked to report on or discuss at a later session. Parents can also cut out this form.

10. Reading Assignment

Ask parents to read "The Family Meeting," Chapter 8 in *The Parent's Handbook*, before the next session. Tell them that this chapter will acquaint them with a procedure for establishing regularly scheduled family meetings in which parents and children make plans, discuss concerns, and share positive experiences and feelings.

Session 8

The Family Meeting

Materials
- *The Parent's Handbook:* Chapter 8, "The Family Meeting"
- Videocassette 2 *or* Audiocassette 5, Side A: "The Family Meeting"
- *Script Booklet*: Session 8 Tapescript
- Discussion Guidelines Poster
- Chart 8: Essentials of Family Meetings

Objectives
This session deals with the purposes and benefits of regularly scheduled family meetings. Parents will learn how to initiate and conduct effective meetings with their children.

Procedures

1. Discussion of the Activity for the Week

Discuss the Activity for the Week from Session 7: Parents were to choose a child-training challenge in which they had unintentionally reinforced a child's misbehavior by doing what the child expected. They were to use the principle of "Acting—Not Reacting." Ask who would like to tell about his or her experiences. Encourage any positive efforts parents have made; it is important to recognize any evidence of progress. If anyone has had difficulty putting a concept into practice, you may want to review the concept briefly.

2. Discussion of the Reading Assignment

The reading assignment for this session was "The Family Meeting," Chapter 8 in *The Parent's Handbook*. Use one of the following procedures to discuss the reading.

Alternative A. You can begin an open discussion by asking, **What did you learn from this reading?** and **How would you apply these ideas?** or, **Do you have any questions about the reading?** This should initiate a discussion that follows the group's interests. Discussion should focus on:

1. What the ideas and principles mean, and

2. Ways to apply these ideas and principles.

Alternative B. If you prefer a more organized format, use the following questions. These questions are supplied as guidelines; they are not intended to limit discussion.

1. What is the authors' definition of a family meeting? Why do they believe family meetings are important?

2. Why do the authors suggest regularly scheduled family meetings rather than meetings only for emergencies?

3. What kinds of things can be discussed in the family meetings?

4. What are the suggested guidelines of the family meeting? Why is each guideline important? For example, why is it important to rotate the chairperson and secretary?

5. What leadership skills are necessary for effective family meetings?

6. When should family meetings be initiated?

7. How do you establish meetings if your spouse is not interested?

8. What are the guidelines for single-parent family meetings?

9. How can family meetings be established with young children?

10. What are some suggested ways of initiating family meetings?

11. What are some common mistakes made in family meetings?

Note: Discussion of Chart 8 follows the presentation of the video or audiocassette. The chart summarizes the material presented on tape.

3. Presentation of Tape

The taped segment for this session is on Videocassette 2 *or* Audiocassette 5, Side A. Turn in your *Script Booklet* to the tapescript for Session 8 and follow the directions for conducting the taped presentation and discussion.

4. Discussion of the Tape

At the end of the tape, a number of people may be ready to ask questions. The preferred method of discussion is to follow topics raised by group members. However, if members are not ready to ask questions, you can begin a discussion with an open question: **What do you think about the ideas we heard and discussed here?**

If your group needs more direction, consider these topics:

a. The purposes of family meetings.

b. The importance of communication skills in family meetings.

c. Various ways to initiate family meetings.

d. The purpose of brainstorming.

e. The rules and procedures of family meetings.

5. Role-Play

Ask for volunteers to role-play their own children in a family meeting. Tell them to describe the children they will play. Then they should describe any other children in the family. Ask for volunteers to play the other children. Ask for two more volunteers to play the parents.

Give the volunteers who play the parents a few minutes to decide on an approach to begin the meeting.

Stop the role-playing after about five minutes and ask the group to analyze the scene.

After discussion, ask other group members to role-play their children and select volunteers for the other roles.

Practice as many family meetings as time permits.

6. Chart 8: Essentials of Family Meetings

Take a few minutes to display and discuss Chart 8, using wording similar to the following:

The statement at the top summarizes the definition and purpose of the family meeting.

The first column gives the guidelines for family meetings. The second column describes common pitfalls to be avoided. Let's discuss each guideline as a review of our discussion of some of the points in our lesson.

Ask: **Why is it important to meet at a regularly scheduled time?**

Continue to discuss each guideline, pointing out the pitfalls to avoid with each one.

7. Problem Situation

The Problem Situation gives parents an opportunity to put this session's ideas into practice. Ask participants to read the Problem Situation at the end of Chapter 8 in *The Parent's Handbook*. Then discuss the questions.

If time permits, you may want to have parents role-play this situation.

8. Summary

The summary is an important part of each session. It gives each parent an opportunity to identify and clarify what she or he is learning. It also gives the leader an opportunity to determine what the parents are learning and to get reactions to the way sessions are being conducted.

The summary may deal either with the session's instructional content or with the feelings of group members about the material.

Begin the summary by asking, **What did you learn from this meeting?** or **What do you think about the ideas presented in this session?**

9. Activity for the Week

For the coming week, ask parents to begin family meetings at home. Tell the group that next week they will have a chance to discuss their experiences.

Remind parents that there are three aids in *The Parent's Handbook* that are designed to help them put the program into practice at home:

- *Chart 8* is included in the handbook to serve as a summary of the major ideas covered in this session.
- *Points to Remember* is a list to remind them of the session's major points. Parents may want to cut it out and post it at home, perhaps on a bulletin board or the refrigerator.
- *My Plan for Improving Relationships* is a form on which parents can write down their concerns and assess their progress. Emphasize that this form is for private use, and is not something they will be asked to report on or discuss at a later session. Parents can also cut out this form.

10. Reading Assignment

Ask parents to read "Developing Confidence and Using Your Potential," Chapter 9 in *The Parent's Handbook*. This final chapter will help participants gain more confidence in their new role as democratic parents.

Developing Confidence and Using Your Potential

Materials

- *The Parent's Handbook:* Chapter 9, "Developing Confidence and Using Your Potential"
- Videocassette 2 *or* Audiocassette 5, Side B: "Building Your Confidence"
- *Script Booklet*: Session 9 Tapescript
- Discussion Guidelines Poster
- Chart 9: Democratic and Positive Parenting
- Pencils and paper

Objectives

This lesson is concerned with helping parents feel more confident in using their new parenting skills. They will learn how to deal with criticism and pressure from others about their new child-training methods. Parents will become more aware of their own assets as well as of their children's assets, and they will examine faulty assumptions that interfere with personal growth. Time will be provided for parents to describe their strengths and to receive encouragement.

Procedures

1. Discussion of the Activity for the Week

Discuss the Activity for the Week from Session 8: Parents were to initiate family meetings. Ask who would like to tell about his or her experiences. Encourage any positive efforts parents have made; it is important to recognize any evidence of progress. If anyone has had difficulty putting a concept into practice, you may want to review the concept briefly.

2. Discussion of the Reading Assignment

The reading assignment for this session was "Developing Confidence and Using Your Potential," Chapter 9 of *The Parent's Handbook.* Use one of the following procedures to discuss the reading.

Alternative A. You can begin an open discussion by asking, **What did you learn from this reading?** and **How would you apply these ideas?** or, **Do you have any questions about the reading?** This should initiate a discussion that follows the group's interests. Discussion should focus on:

1. What the ideas and principles mean, and

2. Ways to apply these ideas and principles.

Alternative B. If you prefer a more organized format, use the following questions. These questions are supplied as guidelines; they are not intended to limit discussion.

1. What is meant by "the rights of both parents and children"?

2. What are the difficulties of giving up your position of power in the family? What are the benefits of giving up this power?

3. The authors believe that the parent, not the child, must be the first to change. What are the implications of this for the challenges parents face with their children?

4. How can unrealistically high standards interfere with effective parent-child relationships?

5. What do the authors suggest we do to avoid becoming discouraged in our relationships with children? What do they mean by setting realistic goals?

6. Why is it important to recognize our strengths that have nothing to do with being a parent? How do you feel about no longer seeing your children as symbols of your success or failure as a person?

7. What are some things we need to consider when others are critical of our child-training methods?

8. What happens when we feel guilty? How can we avoid inappropriate guilt feelings?

9. The authors mention four faulty assumptions which interfere with our personal growth and bring about poor relationships with other people. Do you hold any of these beliefs? Which ones?

10. How can we begin to change these beliefs?

Note: Discussion of Chart 9 follows the presentation of the video or audiocassette. The chart summarizes the material presented on tape.

3. Presentation of Tape

The taped segment for this session is on Videocassette 2 *or* Audiocassette 5, Side B. Turn in your *Script Booklet* to the tapescript for Session 9 and follow the directions for conducting the taped presentation and discussion.

4. Discussion of the Tape

At the end of the tape, a number of people may be ready to ask questions. The preferred method of discussion is to follow topics raised by group members. However, if members are not ready to ask questions, you can begin a discussion with an open question: **What do you think of the ideas we heard and discussed here?**

If your group needs more direction, consider these topics:

a. The consequences of being defensive with a critic.

b. Why many parents are oversensitive to the opinions of others.

c. Why others feel the need to criticize how you raise your children.

d. Taking the blame for our children's liabilities.

e. The futility of trying to prove you're right.

f. Using communication skills to deal with a critic.

g. Dealing with children when your spouse does not agree with your methods.

h. Why grandparents have difficulty understanding the need for new methods of raising children.

i. The consequences for both parent and child when the parent gives in to the child's demands.

j. The solutions presented with each of the situations dramatized in this session.

k. How beliefs and expectations affect one's behavior.

l. The courage to be imperfect.

m. Developing patience.

n. The difference between challenges and problems.

o. Self-defeating patterns in parent-child relationships.

5. Exercise

Ask parents to describe situations in which they have been criticized for their child-training methods.

1. Ask the parent presenting the situation to describe:

    a. How the problem started.

    b. What she or he did.

    c. How the critic responded.

    d. How the situation ended.

2. Ask the group to consider:

    a. The purpose of the critic's behavior.

    b. The purpose of the parent's response.

    c. Why the situation ended as it did.

    d. How the parent might have handled the situation more effectively.

6. Final Exercise

Distribute paper and ask parents to fold their papers and write the following headings on them:

- My personal strengths
- My assets for becoming a more effective parent

Then lead a discussion in which members describe what they see as their own strong points.

After each presentation, ask the rest of the group to comment on other strengths and potentials they believe the person has.

(This final exercise permits group members to clarify the ideas they have developed during the course. It also enables members to encourage each other.)

7. Chart 9: Democratic and Positive Parenting

Take a few minutes to display and discuss Chart 9, using wording similar to the following:

The first column on the left presents typical challenges encountered by parents. The next column describes possible self-defeating beliefs. The third column outlines ineffective, autocratic procedures, while the last column describes positive, democratic procedures.

Go over each example on the chart and then ask: **Do you have any questions about this part of the chart?**

Complete the three examples at the bottom of the chart. Ask: **In the first situation—the child who is resisting going to bed—what might be a typical self-defeating belief of the parent? What would be a typical autocratic procedure? What would be a positive, democratic procedure?**

Repeat this procedure in discussing the other challenges.

8. Problem Situation

The Problem Situation gives parents an opportunity to put this session's ideas into practice. Ask participants to read the Problem Situation at the end of Chapter 9 in *The Parent's Handbook*. Then discuss the questions.

If time permits, you may want to have parents role-play this situation.

9. Summary

The summary is an important part of each session. It gives each parent an opportunity to identify and clarify what he or she is learning, and it gives the leader an opportunity to determine what the parents are learning.

The summary may deal either with the session's instructional content or with the feelings of group members about the material.

Begin the summary by asking, **What did you learn from this meeting?** or **What do you think about the ideas presented in this session?**

10. Concluding the Final Session

You may want parents to identify what they have learned in the STEP program and what specific new attitudes and behaviors they have adopted or plan to adopt.

You may also want parents to evaluate their experience in the program.

Appendix: List of STEP Kit Materials

The complete STEP kit, contained in an easy-to-carry box, consists of:

1 *Leader's Manual*

1 *Parent's Handbook*

***Either* 2 Videocassettes**
Videocassette 1: Introduction to STEP
      The Four Goals of Misbehavior
      Emotions Serve a Purpose
      Encouragement
      Effective Listening
Videocassette 2: Problem Ownership and I-Messages
      Creating Logical Consequences
      Disciplining with Consequences
      The Family Meeting
      Building Your Confidence

***Or* 5 Audiocassettes**
Audiocassette 1, Side A: Introduction to STEP
      Side B: The Four Goals of Misbehavior
Audiocassette 2, Side A: Emotions Serve a Purpose
      Side B: Encouragement
Audiocassette 3, Side A: Effective Listening
      Side B: Problem Ownership and I-Messages
Audiocassette 4, Side A: Creating Logical Consequences
      Side B: Disciplining with Consequences
Audiocassette 5, Side A: The Family Meeting
      Side B: Building Your Confidence

1 *Script Booklet*

1 Discussion Guidelines Poster

10 Charts
Chart 1A The Goals of Misbehavior
   1B The Goals of Positive Behavior
   2 Differences Between the ''Good'' Parent and the Responsible Parent
   3 Differences Between Praise and Encouragement
   4 Effective Listening
   5 Decisions for Effective Communication
   6 The Major Differences Between Punishment and Logical Conse-
      quences

7 Selecting the Appropriate Approach
8 Essentials of Family Meetings
9 Democratic and Positive Parenting

25 Certificates of Participation

Publicity Aids Packet, contained in an envelope, includes
Announcement poster
25 Invitational fliers
Camera-ready ad slicks
Public service announcement
News release
Instructions for using the publicity aids